CONFRONTING
INJUSTICE
WITHOUT
COMPROMISING
TRUTH
STUDY GUIDE

CONFRONTING INJUSTICE WITHOUT COMPROMISING TRUTH

STUDY GUIDE

A GUIDE TO 12 QUESTIONS CHRISTIANS SHOULD ASK ABOUT SOCIAL JUSTICE

THADDEUS J. WILLIAMS

With the Voices of Suresh Budhaprithi, Eddie Byun, Freddy Cardoza,

Becket Cook, Bella Danusiar, Monique Duson, Michelle Lee-Barnewall,

Ojo Okoye, Edwin Ramirez, Samuel Sey, Neil Shenvi, and Walt Sobchak

ZONDERVAN
ACADEMIC

ZONDERVAN ACADEMIC

Confronting Injustice without Compromising Truth Study Guide
Copyright © 2022 by Thaddeus J. Williams

Requests for information should be addressed to:
Zondervan, *3900 Sparks Dr. SE, Grand Rapids, Michigan 49546*

Zondervan titles may be purchased in bulk for educational, business, fundraising, or sales promotional use. For information, please email SpecialMarkets@Zondervan.com.

ISBN 978-0-310-14255-3 (softcover)

ISBN 978-0-310-14257-7 (ebook)

All Scripture quotations, unless otherwise indicated, are taken from the ESV˙ Bible (The Holy Bible, English Standard Version˙). Copyright © 2001 by Crossway, a publishing ministry of Good News Publishers. Used by permission. All rights reserved.

Any internet addresses (websites, blogs, etc.) and telephone numbers in this book are offered as a resource. They are not intended in any way to be or imply an endorsement by Zondervan, nor does Zondervan vouch for the content of these sites and numbers for the life of this book.

Cover design and art: Thaddeus J. Williams

Printed in the United States of America

22 23 24 25 26 27 28 29 30 31 32 33 34 35 /LSC/ 18 17 16 15 14 13 12 11 10 9 8 7 6 5 4 3 2 1

Contents

■ ■ ■ ■

A Word from Thaddeus J. Williams

■ ■ ■ ■

Maybe you are frustrated with a version of Christianity that doesn't seem to take justice seriously. Maybe you are convicted that you haven't taken God's call to justice as seriously as you should and you are looking to grow. Perhaps you have witnessed the rise of ideologies that brand themselves as "social justice," but you have a deep sense that something is profoundly off and maybe even dangerous about them. Perhaps you are seeking biblical clarity on the pressing questions of our day in which most answers seem to come more from rival political agendas and allegiances than from Scripture. Maybe your friendships, your family, and your church home are being torn asunder by social justice controversies and you are looking for healing solutions. Maybe you have a hunch that God offers a better way, a more beautiful and compelling way, to do justice than what's offered by the talking heads on television and the snarky memes on our news feeds.

Welcome to the *Confronting Injustice without Compromising Truth Study Guide*. It is not an exaggeration to say that, as we seek to confront injustice without compromising truth together, we will cover some of the most controversial, combustible, and, I believe, cosmically significant questions of our age. We find on the tip of the iceberg the questions people shout at one another on social media every day—social justice, systemic racism, abortion, sexuality and gender, socialism versus capitalism, red versus blue, us versus them. Underneath that iceberg floats a mass of deeper questions—questions about God, about what it means to be human, what it means for different people to abide together in meaningful community, what it means to be saved, what (or who) is the ultimate source and standard of truth.

Many of us rush straight to the tip-of-the-iceberg questions. They are what pop up on our news feeds. Yet this study plunges under the surface to get at the issues below the issues. And we will explore how Scripture touches and shapes those deeper issues so that we might better heed Paul's Spirit-inspired counsel: "Do not be conformed to this world, but be transformed by the renewal of your mind, that by testing you may discern what is the will of God, what is good and acceptable and perfect" (Romans 12:2).

A Word from John M. Perkins

■ ■ ■ ■

As we dive deeper into the biblical meaning of justice versus its twenty-first-century counterfeits, let us heed the advice of Dr. John M. Perkins, my personal mentor, dear friend, and living legend of the civil rights movement. Dr. Perkins has been working toward justice for over sixty years. He offers the next generation of Christian justice-seekers four nuggets of wisdom as we seek to do justice as Scripture commands:

First, *start with God!* God is bigger than we can imagine. We have to align ourselves with his purpose, his will, his mission to let justice roll down, and bring forgiveness and love to everyone on earth. The problem of injustice is a God-sized problem. If we don't start with him first, whatever we're seeking, it ain't justice.

Second, *be one in Christ!* Christian brothers and sisters—black, white, brown, rich, and poor—we are family. We are one blood. We are adopted by the same Father, saved by the same Son, filled with the same Spirit. In John 17 Jesus prays for everyone who would believe in him, that people from every tongue, tribe, and nation would be one. That oneness is how the world will know who Jesus is. If we give a foothold to any kind of tribalism that could tear down that unity, then we aren't bringing God's justice.

Third, *preach the gospel!* The gospel of Jesus's incarnation, his perfect life, his death as our substitute, and his triumph over sin and death is good news for everyone. It is multicultural good news. In the blood of Jesus, we are able to truly see ourselves as one race, one blood. We've got to stop playing the race game. Christ alone can break down the barriers of prejudice and hate we all struggle with. There is no power greater than God's love expressed in Jesus. That's where we all find real human dignity. If we replace the gospel with this or that man-made political agenda, then we ain't doing biblical justice.

Fourth and finally, *teach truth!* Without truth, there can be no justice. And what is the ultimate standard of truth? It is not our feelings. It is not popular opinion. It is not what presidents or politicians say. God's Word is the standard of truth. If we're trying harder to align with the rising opinions of our day than with the Bible, then we ain't doing real justice.

Those four marks of my sixty years in ministry are exactly what this book is about and why I wholeheartedly stand behind it. Dr. Thaddeus Williams and his twelve coauthors are important voices for helping us pursue the kind of justice that starts with God, champions our oneness in Christ, declares the gospel, and refuses to compromise truth.

We are in the midst of a great upheaval. There is much confusion, much anger, and much injustice. Sadly, many Christian brothers and sisters are trying to fight this fight with man-made solutions. These solutions promise justice but deliver division and idolatry. They become false gospels. Thankfully, in these trying times, new conversations are happening, and the right questions are beginning to be asked. I believe the twelve questions Thaddeus raises in the book are the right questions we should all be asking in today's troubled world.

So I encourage you, read with an open mind. Risk a change of heart. Dare to reach across the divides of our day. Venture beyond anger and hurt into grace and forgiveness. Don't get swept along into false answers that lead only to more injustice. Love one another. Confront injustice without compromising truth—healing, unifying, biblical truth! May this study be a guide to do exactly that, for God's glory and the good of every tongue, tribe, and nation.

John M. Perkins
President Emeritus, John and Vera Mae Perkins Foundation, Jackson, Mississippi
Author of *One Blood*, *Let Justice Down*, and *With Justice for All*

How to Use This Study Guide

■ ■ ■ ■

This study guide was designed to be used in tandem with the *Confronting Injustice without Compromising Truth Video Study*, which offers fourteen sessions and bonus content from notable justice-seekers. For deeper insight, pick up a copy of the book *Confronting Injustice without Compromising Truth*, which features nearly five hundred endnotes that carefully document the controversies covered in these sessions. The book also features seven detailed appendixes covering specific disputes around abortion, racism, capitalism versus socialism, sexuality, culture war, and other topics beyond the scope of this video study.

Each session of this study guide is designed for weekly group gatherings that should take one to two hours and unfolds in five parts:

1. **Word:** Select Scripture passages that set the stage.

2. **Welcome:** A brief word from the author on what to expect.

3. **Watch:** An engaging video message from the author and a message outline.

4. **Wrestle:** A series of questions to help the group process the video's content.

5. **Wrap Up:** A short story from a contributor to add a real-world perspective to the session.

Before embarking on this vital and hopefully transformative study together, we must agree on three ground rules.

Ground rule #1: Let's not fall for the Newman effect.

Since this study guide is designed for group studies, and because we will cross a virtual minefield of cultural controversies, we need to agree on one thing at the outset. Let's make a pact that we will not allow the Newman effect to sabotage our time and growth together. What exactly is the Newman effect?

In 2018 Canadian psychology professor Jordan Peterson joined Channel Four host Cathy Newman to discuss gender inequality in what became one of the most viral interviews of the twenty-first century. The lively exchange sparked the "So you're saying" meme, based on Newman's repeated use of that phrase to interpret Peterson's statements in the most unflattering and inflammatory light possible. "You're saying that women aren't intelligent enough to run these top companies . . ." "You're saying that trans activists could lead to the deaths of millions of people . . ." You're saying that we should organize our societies along the lines of the lobsters . . ."[1]

Professor Peterson wasn't saying any of that. But because his perspective did not fit neatly into the red-and-blue boxes of our day, anything that seemed out of sync with Newman's perspective was taken in the most extreme, cartoonish, and damning way possible.

In a sense, we are all Newmans now, and that has become an existential threat to the unity of the church. "Racism is still a problem." "So you're saying we should abandon the gospel and embrace neo-Marxism!" "The fact that over 70 percent of black children are born without two parents in the home should matter to us!" "So you're saying you're a racist, blaming the victim, and saying the black community's problems are completely their own fault!" "Marriage is a complementary union between a male and a female." "So you're saying you hate gay people." "During the COVID-19 pandemic, we should shelter in place to protect the most vulnerable." "So you're saying you are antifreedom and want us all to bow to tyranny!" "We should reopen the economy to help those whose livelihoods and mental health are being devastated by quarantine." "So you're saying you want the virus to spread and more people to die!" The list could go on and on.

This is what conversations about important questions have reduced to in our day and age. The only way someone could possibly disagree with me is if they are a bad person, a sworn enemy of justice. And so we tar-and-feather any dissonant idea with the worst ideologies we can imagine. The result is rampant self-righteousness and a loss of humble self-criticism, widespread confirmation bias and a loss of real listening required to reach nuanced truths, and pervasive partisanship and a loss of real community that requires us to give charity and the benefit of the doubt to others.

We must resist the Newman effect, especially as Christians. Why? Because regardless of how commonplace and trendy it may be, it is sinful. The Bible commands us not to slander. The Bible commands us to love our neighbors as we ourselves would like to be loved (and who likes to have their views caricatured in the most damning light possible?). The Bible commands us not to bear false witness. The Bible commands us to answer people "with gentleness and respect" (1 Peter 3:15). The Bible commands us not to think of ourselves more highly than we ought to. The Bible commands us to be kind. Tar-and-feathering our brothers and sisters who disagree with us is hardly kind.

So let's make a pact. As we cover controversial topics throughout this study, let's give one another the benefit of the doubt and not play the self-righteous, slanderous game of the Newman effect. This leads us to two more ground rules for our study together.

Ground rule #2: Let's not preach hermit crab theology.

My friend and colleague Rick Langer talks often about what he brands "hermit crab theology." A hermit crab does not have its own shell. It finds some other shell to call home and crams itself inside. Hermit crab theology takes Jesus and jams him inside the preexisting shell of some extrabiblical ideology. This study offers reasons we should never cram Jesus into Leftist ideology, and we should say the same thing about the Right. Why? Because Jesus is too big to fit into the gnarled, cracked shells of any man-made political party. So as we embark on our study, there's a good chance that folks sitting in the same room as you don't share all your political perspectives. So let's agree to take our cues from Jesus and God's Word as we pursue justice together, rather than letting our political allegiances divide us.

Ground rule #3: Let's criticize *ideas* and care for *people*.

Francis Schaeffer, one of the great Christian thinkers and evangelists of the twentieth century, said, "I need to remind myself constantly that this is not a game I am playing. If I begin to enjoy it as a kind of intellectual exercise, then I am cruel and can expect no real spiritual results. As I push the man off his false balance, he must be able to feel that I care for him. Otherwise I will end up only destroying him and the cruelty and ugliness of it all will destroy me as well."[2]

Schaeffer, who spent his career engaging culture, was known to weep often for a generation held captive by bad ideas. In doing so, Schaeffer followed in Paul's footsteps, the apostle who said "with tears" that many "walk as enemies of the cross of Christ" (Philippians 3:18). Schaeffer and Paul imitated Jesus, who saw people "harassed and helpless, like sheep without a shepherd" (Matthew 9:36) and wept over Jerusalem (Luke 19:41–44).

In this study we will wrestle through ideas that have real consequences for real people. Let me be clear: this study takes aim at certain *ideas* but never *people*. It takes aim only at certain ideas because they hurt people we are called to love. Please don't use anything said here to attack *other people*. If we play by the rules of our current cultural moment, then our study will be little more than a self-righteous exercise in dehumanizing those we disagree with—expanding the chasm between a tribalized "us" and a demonized "them." It is easy to be tickled by this or that problem in someone else's ideology. It requires supernatural help to be genuinely concerned that fellow image-bearers, made to know and enjoy God, have been taken in by bad ideas.

With these three ground rules in place—don't fall for the Newman effect, don't practice hermit crab theology, and criticize ideas while caring for people—let's jump into our first session together.

If you have the book this study is based on, *Confronting Injustice without Compromising Truth*, read "What Is 'Social Justice'?" before the first week's session.

What Is "Social Justice"?

■ ■ ■ ■

Open in prayer. Play the video "Confronting Injustice—Introduction."

Word

After watching the short introduction video, let's begin our time together in the Word of God. Open with prayer, then have volunteers read the following four passages aloud:

What does the LORD require of you

but to do justice, and to love kindness,

and to walk humbly with your God? (Micah 6:8)

Then shall your light break forth like the dawn,

and your healing shall spring up speedily. . . .

If you pour yourself out for the hungry

and satisfy the desire of the afflicted,

then shall your light rise in darkness

and your gloom be as the noonday. (Isaiah 58:8, 10)

He judged the cause of the poor and needy;

then it was well.

> Is not this to know me?
>> declares the Lord. (Jeremiah 22:16)

> When you spread out your hands,
>> I will hide my eyes from you;
> even though you make many prayers,
>> I will not listen;
>> your hands are full of blood. . . .
> Cease to do evil,
>> learn to do good;
> seek justice,
>> correct oppression;
> bring justice to the fatherless,
>> plead the widow's cause. (Isaiah 1:15–17)

Welcome

According to the inspired passages we just read, God does not suggest, he commands that we do justice. Doing justice brings a brightness and blessing into our lives. Defending the cause of the poor and needy is what it means to know God. Apathy toward the oppressed can actually hinder our prayers. In short, God takes justice seriously, and so should we.

But what about so-called social justice? Combining the word *social* with the word *justice* is a bit like dropping Mentos into a bottle of soda. It can be highly explosive. Though the term was originally coined by an Italian priest named Luigi Taparelli in the nineteenth century, it has since taken on new meanings, often meanings that stand in contradiction to the historic Christian faith. Journalist Jonah Goldberg shares, "I put on my prospector's helmet and mined the literature for an agreed-upon definition of social justice. What I found was one deposit after another of fool's gold. From labor unions to countless universities to gay rights groups to even the American Nazi Party, everyone insisted they were champions of social justice."[1]

When groups like Antifa, which sees physical violence against those who think differently as "both ethically justifiable and strategically effective," and groups like the American

Nazi Party both claim the moniker of "social justice," then as Christians across the spectrum, we can certainly agree on one thing: *Certain ideologies branding themselves as "social justice" are a far cry from the kind of justice God calls us to in the pages of Scripture.* It is our Christian duty to both expose such doomed ideologies and also embody a more beautiful and compelling and biblical justice before the watching world. In this section we will draw some important distinctions that will help us to do precisely that.

Watch

Play session 1, "What Is 'Social Justice'?" As you watch, use the outline below to follow along and take notes on key insights.

- **People mean very different things by the term *social justice*. What does the Bible say?**

- **God does not suggest, he commands that we do justice.**

    Jeremiah 22:3

    Micah 6:8

    Isaiah 58:6

- **Doing justice will bring blessing into our lives.**

    Isaiah 58:8, 10

- **Doing justice is what it means to know God.**

    Jeremiah 22:16

- **Apathy toward the oppressed can sever our connection with God.**

    Isaiah 1:15–17

    Jeremiah 7:5

- **God's command to *truly* execute justice presupposes that there are ways to execute justice that we think are helpful but are actually hurtful.**

- **There's a big difference between what we might call "Social Justice A" and "Social Justice B" (think *A* for "*awesome*" and *B* for "*bad*" if it helps you remember).**

- **Historic examples of Social Justice A include the following:**
  - Ancient brothers and sisters rescued and adopted the precious little image-bearers who had been discarded like trash, often simply for being female, at the dumps outside many Roman cities.[2]
  - Our Christians brothers and sisters throughout history built more hospitals and orphanages to serve the suffering than any other movement in history, while offering a robust framework for human rights and human sexuality that has brought freedom and dignity to millions.[3]
  - Christians brought skyrocketing literacy rates around the world, even introducing written languages into cultures that had none and spearheading linguistic breakthroughs in modern English, French, and German.
  - Christians through history inspired universities into existence, including St. Andrews, Oxford, Cambridge, Harvard, Princeton, and many more, along with sparking the scientific revolution under the conviction that science exists "to the glory of God and the benefit of the human race."[4]
  - Sophie Scholl's White Rose Society, along with Dietrich Bonhoeffer's and the Confessing Church's resistance movement worked to subvert Hitler's Third Reich.
  - William Wilberforce and the Clapham Sect worked tirelessly to topple slavery in the UK, as did Frederick Douglass, Sojourner Truth, Harriet Tubman, and others in the US. Christians led the movement to abolish slavery not only in America and the United Kingdom but also in India, Africa, Brazil, the Ottoman Empire, and South America.[5]

- **Believers practicing Social Justice A and serving their communities aren't mere relics of the past.**
  - Practicing Christians in the US outpace all other groups in providing food to the poor, donating clothing and furniture to the poor, praying for the poor, and giving personal time to serve the poor in their communities, according to a 2018 study.[6]
  - A dozen faith communities around Philadelphia generated $50,577,098 in economic benefit to their neighborhoods in a single year.[7]
  - Christian communities today excel in adoption, foster parenting, fighting human trafficking, and community development.

- **The Newman effect: "So you're saying . . ."**

Wrestle

To better internalize and act on what you just watched, choose three of the five questions below to wrestle through as a group.

1 Write down the top two or three insights you gained from this session, and briefly share one with the group.

2 Do you think you fall for the Newman effect? If so, how specifically?

3 What two or three things do you hope to gain from this study?

4 Do you hold any political presuppositions that might hinder or derail open group discussions?

5 On a scale of one to ten (one being terrible and ten being awesome), how well do you think you are currently living out God's command (not suggestions) to do justice?

Wrap Up

If you haven't already gone over the three ground rules in "How to Use This Study Guide," do that together now.

Close in prayer.

> If you have the book *Confronting Injustice without Compromising Truth*,
> read chapter 1, "The God Question," before next week's session.

The God Question

■　■　■　■

Does our vision of social justice take
seriously the godhood of God?

Word

Let's begin our time together in the Word of God. Open with prayer, then have volunteers
read the following four passages aloud:

> The Rock, his work is perfect,
>> for all his ways are justice.
> A God of faithfulness and without iniquity,
>> just and upright is he. (Deuteronomy 32:4)

> Although they knew God, they did not honor him as God or give thanks to him, but they
> became futile in their thinking, and their foolish hearts were darkened. Claiming to
> be wise, they became fools, and exchanged the glory of the immortal God for images
> resembling mortal man and birds and animals and creeping things. (Romans 1:21-23)

> You shall have no other gods before me. (Exodus 20:3)

> The LORD is a God of justice. (Isaiah 30:18)

Welcome

Much of the confusion about justice today stems from the fact that we don't start where we should—with God himself. When we don't start with the Creator, all we have are creatures competing for power with their rival, imperfect whims about justice.

Imagine your group has decided to start a meter stick company. It would be a good idea to send a delegate or two from your group on a trip to Paris. (Any volunteers?) Why Paris? Because the City of Light is home to a small piece of engraved marble called the *mètre étalon*, the only official standard meter from the French Revolution that remains in place. This object represents the world standard for the meter. What if, instead of producing meter sticks based on the official standard, your new company chose to cut costs by making *shorter* meter sticks. Then a competing company sees what you are doing and decides to make their meter stick even shorter to reduce overhead and gain an edge over you. With competing meter sticks of varying lengths, everyone slowly forgets about the existence of the *mètre étalon*, and chaos ensues. Some meter sticks could be the length of your pinky finger, some an arm's length, and others could be the length of a football field. It's crazy, right?

God is the *mètre étalon* of justice. He is the standard. But many today have taken a sledgehammer to the marble. All that is left when we reject God as the standard of justice is our individual opinions and various social tribes contriving their own finite versions of justice and competing for power, sometimes violently, to enforce their own brands of "justice." The result is an exhausting and often destructive power play. In this session we will ask whether our vision of social justice takes seriously the godhood of God.

Watch

Play session 2, "The God Question." As you watch, use the outline below to follow along and take notes on key insights.

- **Start with God.**

- **Justice has been defined for millennia as giving others what is due them.** What does it mean to give God, the ultimate other, what he is due?

- **Tenochtitlan (today's Mexico City) is a case study in not giving God his due.**

- **Scripture explains what occurred in Tenochtitlan.** Both the Aztecs and the conquistadors did "what ought not to be done. They were filled with all manner of unrighteousness, evil, covetousness, malice. They are full of envy, murder, strife, deceit, maliciousness" (Romans 1:28–29).

- **We need to start with God to truly understand the nature of injustice, which is the failure to give the Creator his due, swapping Creator for creation worship (Romans 1:19–22).**

- **Look deep enough underneath any human-against-human injustice and you will always find a human-against-God injustice, a refusal to give the Creator the worship only the Creator is due.**

- **All injustice is a violation of the first commandment to have no gods before God.** Acknowledging that God is God—and that the universe, physical sensations, shiny objects, government, and our own desires are not—is where real justice starts.

- **A skeptic's objection:** "If you're saying that the injustices people commit against each other are really failures to give God his due, then why are many culprits of injustice the very people who worship the God of the Bible?"

- **Paul's vision of injustice calls our bluffs.** It reveals what we *actually* worship regardless of what we *say* we worship. Yes, the conquistadors *claimed* to worship the God of the Bible. But their unjust actions falsified their claims. Their envy, strife, deceit, and maliciousness exposed them for what they were—not Creator-worshipers but creation-worshipers groveling on their knees to the false gods of power and profit.

- **If we treat others unjustly, then we too are on our knees to creation rather than the Creator.**

- **If our vision of social justice does not take the godhood of God seriously, then it is not really social justice.**

Wrestle

To better internalize and act on what you just watched, choose three of the five questions below to wrestle through as a group.

1 Which points from the video session resonated with you most profoundly? Write down the top two or three insights you gained from this session, and briefly share one with the group.

2 How much of your justice-seeking energy is focused on giving God his due as your Creator and Redeemer? What are three ways our justice efforts would look different from today's popular visions of social justice if we made revering God the number one priority?

3 What is something you could do every day this week to demonstrate true reverence for God? What long-term habits could you form to orient your life around glorifying God first?

4 Why do you think God *commands* rather than *suggests* that we do justice? What do such commands have to do with God's character, with our chief end to glorify him, and with the mission of the church?

5 What can you do this week to apply the truths of this session as you seek to truly execute justice as Scripture commands?

Wrap Up

Have someone read Eddie's story out loud, then answer the closing question.

I loved every part of pastoring in South Korea. But in the fall of 2010, in the alleyways in Gangnam, I found that thousands of young women had been forced into sexual slavery.

Scripture is crystal clear—the deeply vulnerable are deeply valuable to God. Taking our cues from God's character and commands, our church moved into those areas of vulnerability, looking for ways to serve. We helped rescue a fifteen-year-old named Jinny, who had been violated by a close relative at the age of six. The abuse continued until she was ten. That's when she decided that the streets might be safer than her home. Within hours of her running away, an online trafficker lured Jinny into his home. From that day, she was abused ten to fifteen times a night for the next five years. By God's grace, she was able to run away and find our aftercare center. Jinny had felt worthless her entire life. But through the love and words of her new caregivers, she experienced unconditional love for the first time.

"Why do you care about us?" That was the most common question we would get from those whom society treated as mere sex objects. It was also the easiest question to answer. "We love you because God loves you. We love you because we love God. And God loves you infinitely more than we ever could!" We could credibly verbalize the gospel with them because they could see how the gospel had reshaped our lives.

God empowered us to change fifteen laws in Korea concerning human trafficking and adoption and allowed us to shine light into some of the darkest places on earth. We discovered justice as a way of loving God by imitating the passions of his heart. We wanted to love what he loves. God says point-blank, "I the Lord love justice" (Isa. 61:8). God's heart beats with a passion for the vulnerable in our communities. So should ours.

In some ways, justice seems trendy in our day. But for the believer, we must remember that justice is not a fad; it is the foundation of God's throne (Ps. 89:14). And the One who sits on that throne is the One we seek to honor, love, and follow all our days. Let's start by giving God his due so that we may "truly execute justice one with another" (Jer. 7:5).

Eddie Byun is an associate professor of Christian ministries at Biola University's Talbot School of Theology and author of the award-winning book *Justice Awakening: How You and Your Church Can Help End Human Trafficking* (InterVarsity, 2014).

Which points from this week's session does Eddie's story help to reinforce and deepen, and how can you live out those insights this week in your pursuit of justice?

Close your session in prayer.

> If you have the book *Confronting Injustice without Compromising Truth*, read chapter 2, "The *Imago* Question," before next week's session.

The *Imago* Question

■　■　■　■

Does our vision of social justice acknowledge the image of
God in everyone, regardless of size, shade, sex, or status?

Word

Let's begin our time together in the Word of God. Open with prayer, then have volunteers
read the following four passages aloud:

> God created man in his own image,
>> in the image of God he created him;
>> male and female he created them. (Genesis 1:27)

> What is man that you are mindful of him,
>> and the son of man that you care for him?

> Yet you have made him a little lower than the heavenly beings
>> and crowned him with glory and honor. (Psalm 8:4-5)

> By this it is evident who are the children of God, and who are the children of the devil:
> whoever does not practice righteousness is not of God, nor is the one who does not love
> his brother. (1 John 3:10)

May the Lord make you increase and abound in love for one another and for all.
(1 Thessalonians 3:12)

Welcome

One of the unique and important truths of the Christian worldview is that every human being is a precious image-bearer of the creator of the universe. This fact bestows value, dignity, and worth on everyone—literally *everyone*.

If we treat others as anything less than the image-bearers of God they are, then we aren't engaged in real, God-honoring justice. We are guilty of perpetrating injustice if we treat others as less than ourselves on the basis of the melanin in their skin cells, whether they have XX (female) or XY (male) chromosomes, whether they vote blue or red, whether they have several digits in their bank accounts or nothing at all, or whether they are big enough to play in the NBA or small enough to fit in a thimble. Our worth comes from God, not our size, shade, status, or sex.

Yet there are powerful movements in our culture today, some of which market themselves as advancing the cause of "social justice," that seek to assemble and divide humanity into a hierarchy of groups: groups of more or less value, groups we should revere and groups we should revile, groups who should be "centered" and groups who should be silenced. True Christianity refuses to play the game of group identity hierarchies.

In this session we will ask whether our vision of social justice acknowledges the image of God in everyone, regardless of size, shade, sex, or status.

Watch

Play session 3, "The *Imago* Question." As you watch, use the outline below to follow along and take notes on key insights.

- **Racism is unjust because it elevates skin tone above the Creator.** It is a vertical sin (creature against Creator) in addition to a horizontal (creature against creature) sin.

- **Walt was delivered from racism by the power of the gospel and the doctrine of God's image.**

- **Charles Taylor's immanent frame.** This mark of our secular age is the idea that we inhabit a closed box, a universe unto itself. If we don't believe in a God above and beyond the box, who made the box, then we begin to categorize people by inside-the-box categories like skin tone, sex, size, social status, and so on.

- **If God is dead, then morality dies with him, according to atheists Jacques Monod, Arthur Leff, Jean-Paul Sartre, Alex Rosenberg, and others.**

- **If we are merely our bodies, then there is no meaningful foundation for affirming human equality and value.**

- **As in Martin Luther King Jr.'s "Letter from a Birmingham Jail," we need an outside-the-box, theistic understanding of humanity.**

- **Image-bearer thought experiment.** The people you disagree with most still bear the *imago Dei.*

Wrestle

To better internalize and act on what you just watched, choose three of the five questions below to wrestle through as a group.

1 Which points from the video session resonated with you most profoundly? Write down the top two or three insights you gained from this session, and briefly share one with the group.

2 Why is it sometimes difficult to see people as divine image-bearers? Why does this make Paul's prayer for Christians to "increase and abound in love" so important for us to pray ourselves?

3 Are there any individuals you have a challenging time seeing and treating as image-bearers? For you personally, what might it look like to start treating them as divine image-bearers?

4 Are there any groups defined by inside-the-box categories—race, political persuasion, mental or physical disability, economic status, religion, and so on—that you tend to look down on? What can you do this week to show love for anyone in those groups?

5 What can you do this week to apply the truths of this session as you seek to truly execute justice as Scripture commands?

Wrap Up

Have someone read Walt's story out loud, then answer the closing question.

We were predominantly Americans, but our family backgrounds were Anglo, Irish, Scottish, Russian, Czech, Danish . . . so long as you were not Jewish, you were all right. Socially, we were poor kids who grew up as skinheads, wealthy Mormons, lonely divorced women, and dedicated husbands. Religiously, we were predominantly godless, but what brought us together was the ideology of white supremacy. Reflecting back on this point in my life is quite surreal. Had you asked me ten years ago if I detested *any* group of people, I would have wholeheartedly exclaimed, "No!" Yet I ended up in a racist hate group. How on earth did I get there?

I, and many of the predominantly young men with me, felt forced into a corner. From our public institutions and the culture writ large, we had all heard something to the effect of "Well, you all deserve what's coming to you" or "Well, you can't have an opinion about that" or "Well, you must be racist" or "Well, these other peoples might be worth protecting, but you are expendable." The constant stigma about being white leads young men right into the arms of radicals. Invert everything I said, and you get a radical leftist. "You wanna play the identity politics game? Fine, let's play. We'll win!" seems to be the message coming from both sides of the political spectrum.

How did I escape this hopeless game? I can't think of a specific time or place in which I surrendered to God's grace. But if I were to talk to a younger version of myself, I would say this: "Your value is not rooted in creation but in the Creator. Your value is not rooted in the coincidental happenstance surrounding your birth but in infinite love from he who is Love." For anyone swept into identity politics, right or left, I realize simply saying "Jesus loves you" may not help you stop feeling bad about the world. But don't fall into the trap of defining your life mission by how other people may see you. Define your life on the basis of God who knows and loves you enough to literally *die* for you. How can we see God crucified for every tongue, tribe, and nation and still think ourselves worthy because of our own melanin or merit?

Dear friends who may feel estranged and angry, come and achieve your long-sought revolution! Revolt against your own sin nature. Revolt against hate. Let God graciously turn your heart of stone into a heart of flesh. Look to Jesus and be saved!

Walt Sobchak graduated from Biola University and is currently studying for lifelong ministry.

Which points from this week's session does Walt's story help to reinforce and deepen, and how can you live out those insights this week in your pursuit of justice? Discuss and close your session together in prayer.

If you have the book *Confronting Injustice without Compromising Truth*, read chapter 3, "The Idolatry Question," before next week's session.

The Idolatry Question

■ ■ ■ ■

Does our vision of social justice make a false god
out of the self, the state, or social acceptance?

Word

Let's begin our time together in the Word of God. Open with prayer, then have volunteers
read the following four passages aloud:

> To whom will you liken me and make me equal,
>> and compare me, that we may be alike?
> Those who lavish gold from the purse,
>> and weigh out silver in the scales,
> hire a goldsmith, and he makes it into a god;
>> then they fall down and worship!
> They lift it to their shoulders, they carry it,
>> they set it in its place, and it stands there;
>> it cannot move from its place.
> If one cries to it, it does not answer
>> or save him from his trouble.

> Remember this and stand firm,
>> recall it to mind, you transgressors,
>> remember the former things of old;
> for I am God, and there is no other;
>> I am God, and there is none like me. (Isaiah 46:5-9)

Therefore, my beloved, flee from idolatry. (1 Corinthians 10:14)

I appeal to you therefore, brothers, by the mercies of God, to present your bodies as a living sacrifice, holy and acceptable to God, which is your spiritual worship. Do not be conformed to this world, but be transformed by the renewal of your mind, that by testing you may discern what is the will of God, what is good and acceptable and perfect. (Romans 12:1-2)

You adulterous people! Do you not know that friendship with the world is enmity with God? Therefore whoever wishes to be a friend of the world makes himself an enemy of God. (James 4:4)

Welcome

John Calvin famously observed that the human heart is an idol factory. Fallen human nature constantly cranks out new objects of worship in place of our Creator. But we rarely recognize our idols for what they are. At different stages of my life, I would say, "I'm using my God-given mind to study theology," "I'm just looking for full-time employment doing what I love," "I simply want to buy a home for my family," "My wife and I want another child," or "I am writing another book." The truth is that I turned each of those good things into something ultimate. My sense of self was more wrapped up in these finite pursuits than in the infinite God of the universe. My heart is an idol factory, and if it weren't for Jesus taking my place on the cross, I would be on the eternal receiving end of divine justice for my sin of worshiping and serving created things rather than my Creator.

Idolatry happens when we make a good thing an ultimate thing, turning that good thing into a destructive thing. Given our tendency to make good things into ultimate things, it would be naive to think that idolatry can't creep into our pursuit of justice. How might our false gods skew our vision of justice? What are the idols of our age, on both the Right and the Left, that keep us from truly seeking justice that honors God?

In this session we will ask whether our vision of social justice makes a false god out of the self, the State, or social acceptance.

Watch

Play session 4, "The Idolatry Question." As you watch, use the outline below to follow along and take notes on key insights.

- **Our hearts are idol factories (Calvin).**

- **Some idols are more commonly found on the Right,** including the following:
  - **The idol of stuff:** Material prosperity for its own sake—hoarding wealth and celebrating reckless consumption without regard for the corrosive effects that too much stuff can have on our souls and our society.

  - **The idol of status quo:** Accepting the way things are with no recognition of how many are languishing and the urgent need to bring the lordship of Jesus to bear in such tragic spaces.

- **The idol of solitude:** The kind of rugged individualism by which we think every man is an island unto himself instead of seeing ourselves and our actions as inevitably impacting those around us. It cares only about what Francis Schaeffer called those two "horrible values" of "personal peace and affluence," with blinders on to the oppressed.

- **The idol of sky:** Versions of Christianity in which the whole point is to simply float off into the clouds after we die. The lordship of Jesus extends to every square inch of reality, as Abraham Kuyper noted. That includes poverty, race, sexuality, and politics. A super-spiritualized Christianity that has no implications for real pain in the here-and-now is hardly worthy of the word *Christian*.

- **The idol of skin tone:** This is the point at which the Right becomes the "Alt-Right." Claims to racial superiority have no place whatsoever in a Christian view of the world. We must work to make them a *permanent* thing of the past, never to be resurrected.

The cross and the swastika cannot coexist without one burning up the other.

–Russell Moore

Given God's vision for salvation of every tongue, tribe, and nation, heaven would be a white supremacist's hell.

–Matt Smethurst

- **Some idols are more commonly found on the Left, often disguised as "social justice."**

  > Human beings need religion, they need a religious perspective, a cosmic perspective. And getting rid of the orthodox religions because they were too conservative has simply led to [a] new religion . . . political correctness.[1]
  >
  > −Camille Paglia

  > Critical race and gender theory and postmodernism, the bastard children of Herbert Marcuse and Michel Foucault−have become the premises of higher education, the orthodoxy of a new and mandatory religion.[2]
  >
  > −Andrew Sullivan

  > [Intersectionality is] a quasi-religious gnostic movement, which appeals to people for precisely the reasons that all religions do: It gives an account of our brokenness, an explanation of the reasons for pain, a saving story accompanied by strong ethical imperatives, and hope for the future. In short, it gives life meaning.[3]
  >
  > −Elizabeth Corey

- **Common idols of the Left include the following:**
  - **The idol of self:** Eighty-four percent of Americans believe "enjoying yourself is the highest goal of life." Eighty-six percent believe that to enjoy yourself you must "pursue the things you desire most." Ninety-one percent affirm the statement "To find yourself, look within yourself."[4]

    Making an idol out of the self—the call to follow our hearts and be true to ourselves—is just plain mean. We were never designed to bear the God-sized weight of creating and sustaining our own identities. It deprives us of the unspeakable joy and meaning that go with being authored by Someone far more brilliant, strong, and loving than we are.

○ **The idol of State:**

Once we abolish God, the government becomes God.[5]

–G. K. Chesterton

For deeply spiritual reasons, not merely political ones, people seek universal celebration of their constructed identities. We all need justification, and if we don't find that "not guilty" sentence in Christ, our *parakletos*, or defense attorney, we will seek it in politics and government.

○ **The idol of social acceptance:** We often care more about offending fellow creatures than we do about offending the Creator, and we let that inverted emotion determine the way we think about everything from social policy to sexuality. We often care more about being on "the right side of history"—as the culture's trendsetters define "right"—than we care about being on the right side of Scripture.

You're begging the world for its love. It will not love you back.[6]

–David French

You will be hated by all for my name's sake.

–Jesus in Matthew 10:22

Wrestle

To better internalize and act on what you just watched, choose three of the five questions below to wrestle through as a group.

1 Which points from the video session resonated with you most profoundly? Write down the top two or three insights you gained from this session, and briefly share one with the group.

2 Of the idols explored in this session—status quo, stuff, solitude, sky, skin tone, self, state, sex, and social acceptance—which are you most likely to bow down to? Do any other idols in your life or in the broader culture distort your vision of true justice?

3 Regarding the idol of social acceptance, consider this scenario: What if God's Word clearly said something that was so culturally unpopular, something considered so backward, that you would be called unsavory names, lose your job, and be shunned by your neighbors. Be honest with yourself. Would you side with the masses or the maker of heaven and earth?

4 What metrics could we use to discern when we have crossed the line and turned our political convictions or affiliations into idols? Give an example of what this might look like.

5 What can you do this week to apply the truths of this session as you seek to truly execute justice as Scripture commands?

Wrap Up

Have someone read Becket's story out loud, then answer the closing question.

I spent fifteen years working in Hollywood. I attended the Oscars, Emmys, and Golden Globes. I spent summers in Drew Barrymore's pool and having dinner parties at movie stars' houses. I also knew from an early age that I was attracted to the same sex. But growing up in Dallas in the 1980s, being gay wasn't an option. Through my late teens and early twenties, I found other young gay men who helped me finally feel comfortable in my own skin. This was who I was, and nothing was going to change that. As the glamorous years in Los Angeles went by, I had my share of boyfriends, attended annual pride parades, and marched in rallies for gay marriage. After more than a decade of decadence, I wondered, "Is that all there is?"

In March 2009, I was at Paris Fashion Week, sipping champagne with the who's who of the fashion world. I felt an overwhelming sense of emptiness. I knew that the life I was living couldn't sustain me. I needed answers, but becoming a Christian was out of the question.

Six months later I was at an LA coffee shop with my best friend. We noticed a nearby group of millennials with Bibles on the table. I asked what their church believed about homosexuality, and they answered frankly, that they believed it is a sin. Five years earlier I would have snap-judged them as bigots. Instead, I was able to hear their perspective and thought, "Maybe I'm wrong. What if I've built my life on a false foundation?" They invited me to church.

I found myself in an evangelical church in Hollywood the following Sunday. Every word from the pastor's mouth rang true. *This is the gospel?* It turned everything I had understood about religion on its head. The Holy Spirit overwhelmed me. I began bawling uncontrollably. I knew God was real, Jesus was his Son, heaven was real, the Bible was true—all in an instant. I also knew homosexual behavior was a sin. I knew being gay was no longer who I was. It was part of my past. But I didn't care. I had just met the King of the Universe—Jesus—and his love is all-consuming. Ten years later, I am still single and celibate and have never been happier. I am more than willing to deny myself, take up my cross, and follow Jesus. He's worth it.

What happens when we make sexual desires the supreme markers of our identity? What happens when we sacrifice the truths of God's Word on the altar of cultural trends? We tell the lie that Jesus is not worth it. We do not give the Creator his due, and that is not justice.

Becket Cook is a graduate of Biola University's Talbot School of Theology and author of *A Change of Affection: A Gay Man's Incredible Story of Redemption* (Thomas Nelson, 2019).

Which points from this week's session does Becket's story help to reinforce and deepen, and how can you live out those insights this week in your pursuit of justice? Discuss and close your session in prayer.

Suggested Prayer to Worship
Jehovah over Jezebel

God,

As we seek to obey your commands to do justice in the world, help us keep the first commandment to have no gods before you. When we don't exalt you, when glorifying and enjoying you is not our highest aim every day, when our inescapable, built-in impulse to worship veers from you—our Creator—to creation, then our justice becomes injustice. We don't give you your due. We don't give your image-bearers what they are due. Forgive us for our idolatry. We have bowed to the false gods of stuff, solitude, sky, the status quo, the self, the state, and social acceptance. Help us worship you in Spirit and in truth, that we might become true agents of justice in the world. Amen.

If you have the book *Confronting Injustice without Compromising Truth*, read chapter 4, "The Collective Question," before next week's session.

The Collective Question

■　■　■　■

Does our vision of social justice take any
group-identity more seriously than our
identities "in Adam" and "in Christ"?

Word

Let's begin our time together in the Word of God. Open with prayer, then have volunteers read the following four passages aloud:

> None is righteous, no, not one;
>> no one understands;
>> no one seeks for God.
> All have turned aside; together they have become worthless;
>> no one does good,
>> not even one. (Romans 3:10-12, citing Psalm 14)

> Now in Christ Jesus you who once were far off have been brought near by the blood of Christ. For he himself is our peace, who has made us both one and has broken down in his flesh the dividing wall of hostility. (Ephesians 2:13-14)

There is neither Jew nor Greek, there is neither slave nor free, there is no male and female, for you are all one in Christ Jesus. (Galatians 3:28)

There is therefore now no condemnation for those who are in Christ Jesus. (Romans 8:1)

Welcome

Harvard researcher Robert Putnam found that "if you belong to no groups but decide to join one, you cut your risk of dying the next year in half."[1] One famous study found that group-connected people with unhealthy habits like smoking, poor diet, and heavy drinking consistently outlive disconnected people with otherwise healthy lifestyle habits.[2] Pull a leaf off a tree and it dies. Pull a red-hot ember from a fireplace and it turns to ash. Pull a human out of a meaningful group and he or she starts to fall apart. Every "me" needs a "we."

Biblically speaking, the need to live as more than an isolated me is far from trivial. The Bible begins with a series of benedictions, or good words, that God speaks over his creation. Heavens and earth—good. Oceans, clouds, fruit, and animals—good. Then we reach the first malediction, or bad word, God speaks over his creation. "It is not good," says God, "that the man should be alone" (Genesis 2:18). Our Creator, who is community as Father, Son, and Holy Spirit, designed us for meaningful community.[3]

The God-given need for community has been twisted, like everything else, since that catastrophic day in the garden of Eden. Take a good need for community—a desire to belong to a group bigger than our lonesome selves—then add our fallenness to the mix, and what do you get? You get a gang, a mob, a cult, an abusive church, a hate group, or a totalitarian political party—one self-righteous tribe seeking to vanquish all others. This is the dilemma of our century, and indeed every century: *How do we meet our irrepressible God-given need to belong in groups without those groups becoming self-righteous and resorting to full-blown tribal warfare?* The Bible has an answer to that question. So does Social Justice B. Their answers are very different.

How then should we pursue community? How should we think about group identities in a way that doesn't unleash more injustice into the universe? In this session we will ask if our vision of social justice takes any *group identity* more seriously than our *God-given identities* "in Adam" and "in Christ."

Watch

Play session 5, "The Collective Question." As you watch, use the outline below to follow along and take notes on key insights.

- **The worst ideas of the twentieth century.** *Time* magazine polled Americans on the one hundred worst ideas of the twentieth century. Fast food, aerosol cheese, thong underwear for men, plus-size spandex, breast implants, and a purple dinosaur named Barney all made the list. Of 232,919 votes cast, the number one answer was telemarketing.[4]

- **Tribalism is one of the worst ideas of the twentieth century if we calculate by lives lost.** Tribalism sounds like this:

  We are Aryan, we are good; they are Jewish, they are bad.

  We are Brahman class, we are good; they are Untouchables, they are bad.

  We are Hutu, we are good; they are Tutsi, they are bad.

  We are white, we are good; they are black, they are bad.

  We are the Islamic State, we are good; they are infidels, they are bad.

- **Underneath tribalism we find our God-given need for community.** The first malediction God speaks in Scripture, the first bad word, is that it's not good for man to be alone (Genesis 2:18). It is not good for man to be alone because we are created in the image of a triune, relational God. We are created *for* community by a God who *is* community.

- **When that God-given need for community is not met in Christ and the church, we often form gangs, mobs, cults, and other twisted forms of tribalism.** This destructive community-seeking occurs on both ends of the political spectrum.

  Christian Picciolini's story from the Right

  Conor Barnes's story from the Left: "Flee the cult!"

- **Paul faced the problem of bringing togetherness, church, *ekklesia* to different groups in the first century.** He did so by emphasizing two core theological truths:

  1. **All have sinned and fallen short of God's glory (Romans 3:23).** *Paul told the truth that sin is not exclusively the oppressor's problem but a human problem.* Some Jews thought that, by virtue of their Jewishness, they were superior to non-Jews. Paul countered, "What then? Are we Jews any better off? No, not at all. For we have already charged that all, both Jews and Greeks, are under sin" (Romans 3:9).

2. **Being "in Christ Jesus" is a new identity that transcends other group identities.** *Our "in Christ" identity is a wrecking ball through any group-identity-based ideology, Right or Left.*

> In Christ Jesus you are all sons of God, through faith. For as many of you as were baptized into Christ have put on Christ. There is neither Jew nor Greek, there is neither slave nor free, there is no male and female, for you are all one in Christ Jesus. (Galatians 3:26-28)

- **Edwin's story of waking up from wokeness.** "That's my sister in Christ!" "We're family!"

Wrestle

To better internalize and act on what you just watched, choose three of the five questions below to wrestle through as a group.

1 Which points from the video session resonated with you most profoundly? Write down the top two or three insights you gained from this session, and briefly share one with the group.

2 What pressures does the tribalism of our culture place on the church? Where is there a push to conform the church to fit unbiblical notions of community? Try to identify five major differences between what the church is supposed to be according to the New Testament versus what we hear from the various "tribes" of our culture.

3 Does the biblical doctrine of universal human depravity—that all have sinned and fall short of God's perfect standard of goodness and justice—prevent us from falling into tribalism or identity politics on either the Left or the Right? If so, how?

4 What can we as Christians do to live out our shared "in Christ" identity with those from different tongues, tribes, and nations? Share some examples.

5 What might you or others in your group do this week to apply the truths of this session as you seek to truly execute justice as Scripture commands?

Wrap Up

Have someone read Edwin's story out loud, then answer the closing question.

When I was "woke," I did not realize how much resentment I harbored. I had hurt many people and severed friendships. I used my social media platforms to vent my self-righteous indignation toward white America. I imbibed such racist ideas from theologians like James Cone, which left me struggling to see fellow church members as equally loved and embraced by God. Why? Because of the color of their skin. Everything was about racism all the time.

Then the Lord opened my eyes and set me free in an unexpected place, a rural, predominantly white church. Scanning the room, my eyes fell on an older lady whose face was filled with joy as she worshiped our God. Then it hit me: "That older white lady is my sister in the Lord!" Bible passages about the redemptive work of Christ rushed through my mind. I left the church humbled by the reality of my own weakness and utter dependence on Christ. I had been so blinded by an ideology that divided people by skin color that I missed the blessing of seeing the sufficiency of Christ's atonement. Though I considered myself woke, my bitterness toward white people had closed my eyes to God's marvelous saving power in the gospel.

If you're not heavily involved in Social Justice B or the woke movement, don't feel like you are missing out. You aren't. Instead, look to Christ in Scripture. Rather than being versed in the ever-changing cannon of woke literature, aim to be rooted in theological truths and live out biblical unity in the context of your local church.

For those who consider themselves woke, examine your hearts. What effect is reading oppression into all of life having on your soul? What do you see when you encounter a fellow Christian, their "in Christ" identity as your family or whether their appearance places them in the oppressed or oppressor group? Does your wokeness give you a sense of moral superiority or make you utterly dependent on the righteousness of Christ? Do you prejudge people by their melanin, or do you love your brothers and sisters in the Lord with an open heart? I know how a noble desire for justice can replace love in our hearts with resentment. I know because it happened to me. But by God's grace, I have been set free. I pray that you too can exchange the rage of wokeness for the joy of the gospel of Christ, who "himself is our peace, who has made us both one and has broken down in his flesh the dividing wall of hostility" (Eph. 2:14).

Edwin Ramirez hosts the podcast *The Proverbial Life* and blogs regularly at www.theproverbiallife.com.

Which points from this week's session does Edwin's story help to reinforce and deepen, and how can you live out those insights this week in your pursuit of justice?

Discuss and close your session in prayer.

If you have the book *Confronting Injustice without Compromising Truth*, read chapter 5, "The Splintering Question," before next week's session.

The Splintering Question

■ ■ ■ ■

Does our vision of social justice
embrace divisive propaganda?

Word

Let's begin our time together in the Word of God. Open with prayer, then have volunteers read the following four passages aloud:

You shall love your neighbor as yourself. (Matthew 22:39)

You have heard that it was said, "You shall love your neighbor and hate your enemy." But I say to you, Love your enemies and pray for those who persecute you, so that you may be sons of your Father who is in heaven. (Matthew 5:43-45)

Now you must put them all away: anger, wrath, malice, slander, and obscene talk from your mouth. (Colossians 3:8)

If you have bitter jealousy and selfish ambition in your hearts, do not boast and be false to the truth. This is not the wisdom that comes down from above, but is earthly, unspiritual, demonic. For where jealousy and selfish ambition exist, there will be disorder and every vile practice. But the wisdom from above is first pure, then peaceable, gentle, open to reason, full of mercy and good fruits, impartial and sincere. (James 3:14-17)

Welcome

Propaganda has been used throughout history to dupe people into thinking they were doing justice when they were actually unleashing hell on earth. Under the spell of propaganda, people turned their Jewish neighbors over to Hitler's Gestapo, massacred kulaks in the Soviet Union, betrayed Tutsi villagers during the Rwandan genocide, and targeted Christians and Yezidis in the Middle East. Examples could be multiplied ad nauseam. If you can use words and images to paint an entire group of image-bearing human beings as subhuman, then people will commit subhuman acts against them.

Propaganda is utterly contrary to the way of Jesus and God's redemptive vision for every tongue, tribe, and nation. So how can we spot it? What are the marks of propaganda? How can we immunize ourselves against it so we don't join the mob? How does the Bible, with its commands to love our neighbors and even our enemies, help us rise above the mudslinging, stereotyping, and scapegoating rhetoric that is all too common in our age? In this session we will ask whether our vision of social justice embraces divisive propaganda.

Watch

Play session 6, "The Splintering Question." As you watch, use the outline below to follow along and take notes on key insights.

- **Propaganda is the uranium that powers tribalism and the social meltdown it incurs.**
  - An old Nazi pamphlet says that the Jew "only looks human, with a human face, but his spirit is lower than that of an animal. . . . [He represents] unparalleled evil, a monster, subhuman."[1]
  - The Tutsis in Rwanda were called *inyenzi*, or "cockroaches."

- KKK literature reduced blacks in the US to "gorillas."
- The two million victims of Khmer Rouge were deemed "microbes" who must be "swept aside" and "smashed."[2]
- White supremacists of the 2017 Unite the Right rally in Charlottesville spoke of the "parasitic class of anti-white vermin."

• **Three marks of propaganda:** (1) damning revisionist histories, (2) individuals as group exemplars, and (3) scapegoating.

• **Damning revisionist history.** Social Justice B tells us that slavery is the legacy of a particular people group—white, European, imperialistic, and usually Christian males. If that's the story we want to tell, then we must blot many important historical facts from our collective memory. Thomas Sowell documents some of these in his chapter "The Real History of Slavery":
  - "Slavs were so widely used as slaves in both Europe and the Islamic world that the very word 'slave' derived from the word for Slav."[3]
  - "China in centuries past has been described as 'one of the largest and most comprehensive markets for the exchange of human beings in the world.' Slavery was also common in India. . . . [and] an established institution in the Western Hemisphere before Columbus' ships ever appeared on the horizon."[4]
  - "While slavery was common to all civilizations . . . only one civilization developed moral revulsion against it, very late in its history—Western civilization."[5]
  - "The British stamped out slavery, not only throughout the British Empire . . . but also by its pressures and actions against other nations" including Brazil, Sudan, Zanzibar, the Ottoman Empire, and Western Africa.[6]

- ○ "Americans stamped out slavery in the Philippines, the Dutch stamped it out in Indonesia, the Russians in Central Asia, the French in their West African and Caribbean colonies."[7]
- ○ The Westerners who stamped out slavery did so "over the bitter opposition of Africans, Arabs, Asians, and others."[8]
- ○ "Moreover, within Western civilization, the principal impetus for the abolition of slavery came first from very conservative religious activists—people who would today be considered 'the religious right.'"[9]

- **Individuals as group exemplars.**

. . . here in the land of legislatively legitimated toxic masculinity, is it really so illogical to hate men? But we're not supposed to hate them because . . . #NotAllMen . . . but when they have gone low for all of human history, maybe it's time for us to go all Thelma and Louise and Foxy Brown on their collective butts. . . .	Every Hutu should know that every Tutsi is dishonest in business. His only priority is the supremacy of his ethnic group. . . . The experience of the October war has taught us a lesson. . . . The Hutus must be firm and vigilant against their common Tutsi enemy. . . .
[Men should] pledge to vote for feminist women only. Don't run for office. Don't be in charge of anything. Step away from the power. We got this . . .	All strategic positions, political, administrative, economic, military and security should be entrusted only to Hutu. The education sector (schools, pupils, students, teachers) must be majority Hutu. . . .
Growing movements challenge a masculinity built on domination and violence and to engage boys and men in feminism are both gratifying and necessary. Please continue . . .	Hutu ideology must be taught at every level to every Hutu. Every Hutu must spread this ideology widely. . . .
And please know that your crocodile tears won't be wiped away by us anymore. You have done us wrong. #BecausePatriarchy.	The Hutu should stop having mercy on the Tutsi. . . .
It is long past time to play hard for Team Feminism. And win.	The Hutu must be firm and vigilant against their common enemy: the Tutsi.

- **Scapegoating.** Social Justice B projects all our pain on the damnable group and its exemplars.

> I was a depressed and anxious teenager, in search of answers. Radicalism explained that these were not manageable issues with biological and lifestyle factors, they were the result of living in capitalist alienation. . . . The force that causes depression is the same that causes war, domestic abuse, and racism. By accepting this framework, I surrendered to an external locus of control. Personal agency in such a model is laughable. And then, when I became an even less happy and less strong person over the years as an anarchist, I had an explanation on hand.[10]
>
> —Conor Barnes

- **Social Justice B is a theodicy, an attempt to explain the evil and suffering in the universe.** Will playing the group identity game end well for anyone?

- **The Bible offers a better way forward in its command to love our neighbors and its recognition that our core identity is in the grace of God thanks to Christ.**

Wrestle

To better internalize and act on what you just watched, choose three of the five questions below to wrestle through as a group.

1 Which points from the video session resonated with you most profoundly? Write down the top two or three insights you gained from this session, and briefly share one of them with the group.

2 Why is it so easy to blame our life troubles on other people groups? What do you think motivates this impulse?

3 Think of specific people groups who have been made scapegoats in our society today. How can you be countercultural by loving people in those groups this week?

4 One powerful remedy to propaganda is spending time with people who disagree with us, deliberately escaping our echo chambers. What echo chambers are you occupying, and how can you venture beyond them this week? Share some ideas and examples of how you or others in your group might escape the echo chamber.

5 What can you do this week to apply the truths of this session as you seek to truly execute justice as Scripture commands?

Wrap Up

Have someone read Suresh's story out loud, then answer the closing question.

I was born into a destitute Dalit family in Nepal in 1979. A Dalit is known as "Achhut" (Untouchable), a term invented to humiliate the downtrodden. Even dogs are allowed to enter the houses of the upper caste, but not Dalits. We are treated as subhuman.

In the summer of 1999, I had a breakthrough at the Monkey Temple in Kathmandu. I met a theology student on a mission trip. We walked the temple steps for hours, talking about the differences between grace-based Christianity and karma- and caste-based Hinduism. At last, a truly humanizing way to see my identity! That night, I accepted Jesus as my Savior. I found a dignity in the eyes of my Creator who didn't see me as "untouchable" but reached down to love me, embrace me as his son, and offer me "every spiritual blessing in the heavenly places" (Eph. 1:3). Jesus welcomes us regardless of our social status or religious performance!

My dream of being treated with dignity as an image-bearer of God is still a far cry in Nepali society. What is truly scandalous is that Nepali churches are no different. We hear propaganda, even within the church, that "people of lower castes have lower intellectual ability." It makes no difference that I recently earned my master's degree in theology. As a result, Dalits are compelled to either hide their identities or start their own churches.

Instead of mirroring Jesus, who loves every tongue, tribe, and nation, the church has simply gone with the flow of Nepal's caste-based discrimination. Ephesians 2:14 teaches that Jesus has made the Jews and Gentiles one, having broken down the dividing wall of hostility through the cross. Why, then, would we keep intact the dividing wall between non-Dalit and Dalit?

It is time for the church around the world to show what true social justice looks like. We must live out the biblical truth that everyone bears God's image and should be treated as such. We must preach the gospel of Jesus's death and resurrection that gives dignity and worth not only to Dalits in my country but to the downtrodden around the world. We must follow God's command to "show no partiality as you hold the faith in our Lord Jesus Christ" (James 2:1). And finally, we must pray. Pray for the church in Nepal. Pray for the church around the world. Pray that we would truly do justice, because Jesus has turned the walls of hostility into rubble.

Suresh Budhaprithi earned his master of divinity at the Kathmandu Institute of Theology and is continuing his training for lifelong ministry. To help him and his family overcome injustice, search "bless the Budhaprithis" at www.gofundme.com.

Which points from this week's session does Suresh's story help to reinforce and deepen, and how can you live out those insights this week in your pursuit of justice? Discuss and close your session in prayer.

If you have the book *Confronting Injustice without Compromising Truth*, read chapter 6, "The Fruit Question," before next week's session.

The Fruit Question

■ ■ ■ ■

Does our vision of social justice replace love, peace,
and patience with suspicion, division, and rage?

Word

Let's begin our time together in the Word of God. Open with prayer, then have volunteers read the following four passages aloud:

> Let all bitterness and wrath and anger and clamor and slander be put away from you, along with all malice. (Ephesians 4:31)

> If you bite and devour one another, watch out that you are not consumed by one another. (Galatians 5:15)

> Strive for peace with everyone, and for the holiness without which no one will see the Lord. See to it that no one fails to obtain the grace of God; that no "root of bitterness" springs up and causes trouble, and by it many become defiled. (Hebrews 12:14-15)

> The fruit of the Spirit is love, joy, peace, patience, kindness, goodness, faithfulness, gentleness, self-control; against such things there is no law. (Galatians 5:22-23)

49

Welcome

Real community—something we all long for and were created for—does not come easy. Think of how easily our hearts harbor grudges and assume the worst of others to feel better about ourselves and our clans. This is what our hearts do in their fallen default mode. And that is one reason Paul talks so much about *schismata*—the sin of divisiveness (1 Corinthians 1:10)—and why he emphasizes the fruit of the Spirit.

For quick-to-quarrel, easy-to-offend, clique-forming people to experience deep community, we need love, joy, peace, patience, kindness, goodness, gentleness, and self-control to deal with other far-from-perfect people. These "fruits" must be Spirit-produced. Without the Spirit's fruit, we fall back into tribal default mode. That is why any approach to social justice that encourages suspicion and rage instead of the fruit of the Spirit has no place in Jesus's church.

This tribal mentality is one of the primary reasons I wrote this study. After decades of ministry, I saw something strange and disturbing happening to students, friends, and family members. I saw the love, peace, and patience in their lives gradually replaced with suspicion, division, and rage, and it broke my heart. I saw a common thread as well. The culprit often seemed to be a new ideology that each had recently embraced, a Social Justice B ideology that encouraged them to interpret all of life through the lens of the oppressors versus the oppressed. In this session we will ask whether our vision of social justice replaces love, peace, and patience with suspicion, division, and rage.

Watch

Play session 7, "The Fruit Question." As you watch, use the outline below to follow along and take notes on key insights.

- **The fruit of the Spirit is love, joy, peace, patience, kindness, goodness, faithfulness, gentleness, and self-control.** The most authentic love, joy, and peace we have ever experienced are not produced *by* us but produced *in* us *by* the Holy Spirit.

- **Corrie ten Boom experienced the fruit of the Spirit.** She handled injustice with humility, questioning her own feelings and replacing anger with "a flood of healing warmth" from the Holy Spirit.

- **Spirit-powered forgiveness at Emmanuel Church.** This same kingdom shone through the darkness of Dylann Roof's racist shooting spree that left nine precious black image-bearers dead at Emanuel Church in Charleston in 2015. Roof tried to start a "race war." But rather than supplying the reciprocated rage to fuel such a war, those who lost loved ones to Roof's racial hatred responded with forgiveness.

  > You took something really precious from me. I will never talk to her ever again. I will never be able to hold her again, but I forgive you and have mercy on your soul.[1]
  >
  > *—daughter of shooting victim Ethel Lance*

  > I've realized that forgiving is so much tougher than holding a grudge. It takes a lot more courage to forgive than it does to say, "I'm going to be upset about whatever forever." . . . After seeing how people could forgive, I truly hope that people will see that it wasn't just us saying words. I know, for a fact, that it was something greater than us, using us to bring our city together.
  >
  > *—son of shooting victim Sharonda Hughes-Singleton*

  > I would just like him to know that . . . I forgive him and my family forgives him. But we would like him to take this opportunity to repent. Repent. Confess. Give your life to the one who matters most: Christ. So that he can change him and change your ways, so no matter what happens to you, you'll be okay.
  >
  > *—relative of shooting victim Myra Thompson*

I acknowledge that I am very angry. But one thing that DePayne always enjoined in our family . . . is she taught me that we are the family that love built. We have no room for hating, so we have to forgive.

−sister of shooting victim DePayne Middleton Doctor

- **Contrast Ten Boom's and the saints at Emmanuel Church's responses to injustice with that of bell hooks.**

I stare him down with rage, tell him I do not want to hear his liberal apologies, his repeated insistence that "it was not his fault." I am shouting at him that it is not a question of blame, that the mistake was understandable, but that the way K was treated was completely unacceptable, that it reflected both racism and sexism. . . . I let him know he had an opportunity to not be complicit with the racism and sexism that is so all pervasive in this society. . . . I felt a "killing rage." I wanted to stab him softly, to shoot him with the gun I wished I had in my purse. And as I watched his pain, I would say to him tenderly "racism hurts." . . . As though I were the black nightmare that haunted his dreams, he seemed to be waiting for me to strike, to be the fulfillment of his racist imagination. I leaned toward him with my legal pad and made sure he saw the title written in bold print: "Killing Rage."[2]

−bell hooks

- **The Bible commands, not suggests, that we love our enemies (Matthew 5:43–48).** The Holy Spirit, through Paul, commands us to "let all bitterness and wrath and anger and clamor and slander be put away from you, along with all malice. Be kind to one another, tenderhearted, forgiving one another, as God in Christ forgave you" (Ephesians 4:31–32). He also says,

Repay no one evil for evil, but give thought to do what is honorable in the sight of all. If possible, so far as it depends on you, live peaceably with all. Beloved, never avenge yourselves, but leave it to the wrath of God, for it is written, "Vengeance is mine, I will repay, says the Lord." To the contrary, "if your enemy is hungry, feed him; if he is thirsty, give him something to drink; for by so doing you will heap burning coals on his head." Do not be overcome by evil, but overcome evil with good. (Romans 12:17-21)

Wrestle

To better internalize and act on what you just watched, choose three of the five questions below to wrestle through as a group.

1 Which points from the video session resonated with you most profoundly? Write down the top two or three insights you gained from this session, and briefly share one with the group.

2 We all from time to time may experience something like the rage bell hooks expresses in her essay "Killing Rage." In those moments, which Christian truths can we preach to ourselves to replace rage with the kind of grace and love we see in Corrie ten Boom?

3 How do you think preaching the gospel to ourselves every day—reminding ourselves of the amazing grace God extended to us when we were hostile to him—could impact our approach to social justice? How might excluding the good news of God's forgiveness from our daily thought lives and emotions pollute our passion for social justice?

4 In our social media age of daily online warfare and polarization, what are some ways to embody the fruits of the Spirit online with those who disagree with us? Share some examples you have tried or that you have seen others practice.

5 What can you do this week to apply the truths of this session as you seek to truly execute justice as Scripture commands?

Wrap Up

Have someone read Michelle's story out loud, then answer the closing question.

When I was growing up in Minnesota, one of the things that made me acutely aware of being a racial minority was the seemingly endless "So where are you from?" questions. I quickly learned that people didn't want an answer like "Minnesota." They were satisfied only once I said something about my parents being born in Korea. Even though my siblings and I were born in America, meaning this was the only country we knew, we were assumed to be foreigners, which is especially hard as a kid trying to figure out your place in the world.

Anger is easy, but I've learned that's not the only way I can respond. As a graduate student, my friend approached a shop owner who was clearly not white and asked, "So where are you from?" I was horrified. To my astonishment, the man was delighted. He shared story after story about Egypt, the country he loved. When you meet someone, you can't immediately tell whether they will be offended or delighted if you ask where they are from. This taught me the importance of grace in our interactions. As Christians, we are called into deep relationships with one another, but it's hard to do that if we feel like we have to walk on eggshells.

Grace takes our human limitations into account. Do people ever say something to me I don't like? Certainly. I have also said many things others don't like, and they gave me grace. None of us has a monopoly on giving or receiving offensive comments. That's why giving grace has become so important for me personally. Focusing on how I've been offended may make me feel good for a moment, but it also leads me down the path of bitterness that can overtake my soul and trap me in resentment.

The Bible calls us to a love that is not easily offended (1 Cor. 13:5). Grace doesn't mean I think terrible actions are okay, but it compels me to remember that I am relating with someone who is imperfect, like me. If we're going to have productive conversations about controversial social justice topics, we have to be willing to give people space to make honest mistakes. As a follower of Jesus, I am called to build up others in the body instead of shaming them (1 Cor. 14:26). We shouldn't expect instant perfection but realize we are all constantly growing in grace and truth (John 1:17). And we need the Holy Spirit's help to do that (Gal. 5:16-25)!

Michelle Lee-Barnewall served as an associate professor of New Testament at Biola University's Talbot School of Theology and blogs regularly at https://www.biola.edu/blogs/good-book-blog.

Which points from this week's session does Michelle's story help to reinforce and deepen, and how can you live out those insights this week in your pursuit of justice? Discuss and close your session in prayer.

Suggested Prayer to Seek Unity over Uproar

God,

You designed us for community, but in our fallen state, we take the good relational drives you gave us and we twist them into tribalism. Help us humbly recognize our shared fallenness in a way that smashes all claims to ethnic, gender, or economic superiority. Help us to see our "in Christ" identity as infinitely precious so that people from every tongue, tribe, and nation can transcend our grievances and embrace one another as brothers and sisters with whom we will enjoy eternity. Help us see through and stand against vicious propaganda that pretends to be justice but rewrites history, treats individuals as group exemplars, and blames all life's problems on different people groups. Replace suspicion and rage inside us with the life-giving fruit of the Spirit. Fill us with the supernatural love, joy, peace, patience, kindness, goodness, faithfulness, and self-control we need in order to have real unity in your church. Amen.

If you have the book *Confronting Injustice without Compromising Truth*, read chapter 7, "The Disparity Question" before next week's session.

The Disparity Question

■ ■ ■ ■

Does our vision of social justice prefer

damning stories to undamning facts?

Word

Let's begin our time together in the Word of God. Open with prayer, then have volunteers read the following four passages aloud:

Can wicked rulers be allied with you,

those who frame injustice by statute? (Psalm 94:20)

I passed by the field of a sluggard,

by the vineyard of a man lacking sense,

and behold, it was all overgrown with thorns;

the ground was covered with nettles,

and its stone wall was broken down.

Then I saw and considered it;

I looked and received instruction.

A little sleep, a little slumber,

a little folding of the hands to rest,

and poverty will come upon you like a robber,

and want like an armed man. (Proverbs 24:30-34)

Do not judge by appearances, but judge with right judgment. (John 7:24)

It will be like a man going on a journey, who called his servants and entrusted to them his property. To one he gave five talents, to another two, to another one, to each according to his ability. Then he went away. He who had received the five talents went at once and traded with them, and he made five talents more. So also he who had the two talents made two talents more. But he who had received the one talent went and dug in the ground and hid his master's money. (Matthew 25:14-18)

Welcome

The Bible warns us not to be allied with those who "frame injustice by statute" (Psalm 94:20)—that is, those who inject disobedience to God's law into human legal codes. Evil humans make evil laws. We build our sins into our systems.

Heinrich Himmler, Hermann Goering, and Adolf Hitler's sin of anti-Semitism wasn't just individually expressed; it was systematized into ghettos and gas chambers. The sin of antiblack racism wasn't just expressed by individuals; it was framed by statute through the American slave trade, the Supreme Court's infamous Dred Scott ruling, Jim Crow laws, the Alabama statute that required black people to surrender their bus seats to white people (a law Rosa Parks courageously broke), denying GI Bill benefits to black veterans, redlining, and more. The caste system of India, which branded most citizens "untouchable," was an injustice baked into the very systems by which Hindu society functioned. Apartheid in South Africa, China's one-child policy—the list of systemic injustices could go on ad nauseam. The Bible had it right thousands of years ago. We indeed "frame injustice by statute."

But this biblical insight that sin can be supersized and systematized is usually not what Social Justice B means by "systemic injustice." There are important differences. If we don't ponder these differences, the church will find itself bowing down to a trendy ideology rather than to Jesus as Lord. One of those trendy ideologies in our day is a version of Social Justice B that sees any disparity as damning proof of some vicious form of discrimination.

But is this ideology defensible? Is it true? Does it help us pursue true justice? In this session we will ask whether our vision of social justice prefers damning stories to undamning facts.

Watch

Play session 8, "The Disparity Question." As you watch, use the outline below to follow along and take notes on key insights.

- **Is there such a thing as systemic injustice?** Biblically, the answer is yes (e.g., Psalm 94:20, Darius and Nebuchadnezzar's decreed idolatry in the book of Daniel). Historically, the answer is also yes (e.g., the caste system in Nepal and India, apartheid in South Africa, the Nazi regime, Stalin's Russia, American slavery, Jim Crow laws, redlining, etc.).

- **Social Justice B has a very different definition of systemic injustice, namely, that disparity equals discrimination.**

  > Racial disparities must be the result of racial discrimination.[1]
  >
  > –Ibram X. Kendi

- **Racism on the New Jersey Turnpike?** Public Services Research Institute's "study concluded that blacks make up 16 percent of the drivers on the turnpike and 25 percent of the speeders in the 65 m.p.h. zones, where complaints of profiling have been most common."[2] There is a median age difference between white and black drivers, which better explains the disparity (i.e., young people drive faster than old people).

- **Racism in home loans?** Bank lenders across the US rejected twice as many blacks as whites for home loans, 44.6 percent compared with 22.3 percent. The US Commission on Civil Rights report found that white Americans are turned down nearly twice as often as Asian Americans and Native Hawaiians for those same mortgages (22.3 percent versus 12.4 percent).[3]

> Black-owned banks turned down black applicants for home mortgages at a *higher* rate than did white-owned banks.[4]
>
> *–Thomas Sowell*

- **In a discrimination-free world, there would still be disparities based on such undamning factors as geography, calendars, and candles.**

- **Different choices yield different outcomes, according to Scripture.**

> A slack hand causes poverty,
>> but the hand of the diligent makes rich. (Proverbs 10:4)

> In all toil there is profit,
>> but mere talk tends only to poverty. (Proverbs 14:23)

> The sluggard does not plow in the autumn;
>> he will seek at harvest and have nothing. (Proverbs 20:4)

> If anyone is not willing to work, let him not eat. (2 Thessalonians 3:10)

- **Disparities that have nothing to do with discrimination are common.**
  - Twenty-two of the twenty-nine astronauts in the original Apollo space program were firstborns.
  - People living in the US experience 90 percent of the world's tornadoes.
  - Asians are underrepresented in the NBA, NFL, NHL, and MLB.
  - Women are overrepresented in health care, in attaining university degrees, and in setting consumer trends that determine the actions of the world's biggest corporations.
  - Men make up an overwhelming majority of soldiers who perish on battlefields and have a virtual monopoly of the bricklaying, plumbing, and carpentry industries.
  - Jewish people, "being less than 1 percent of the world's population . . . received 22 percent of Nobel Prizes in chemistry, 32 percent in medicine and 32 percent in physics."[5]
  - Conservative Protestants have far less wealth than Catholics and mainline Protestants, with Episcopalians and Jewish Americans earning far above the rest. The median net worth of conservative Protestants came to $26,000 compared with a median net worth of $150,890 for proponents of Judaism.[6]

- **Some disparities are caused by evil discrimination.** Questioning damning explanations is not to side with the oppressors but to seek clarity about the scope of oppression so we can fight the real thing and not a bogeyman.

Wrestle

To better internalize and act on what you just watched, choose three of the five questions below to wrestle through as a group.

1 Which points from the video session resonated with you most profoundly? Write down the top two or three insights you gained from this session, and briefly share one with the group.

2 There is real systemic injustice in our fallen world. Think of three reasons it is important as we seek to love the oppressed that we carefully distinguish between inequalities that are unjust and sinful and those that have other explanations.

3 In many spheres of our culture—in much of our media, entertainment, and higher education—we face serious consequences if we question whether discrimination is the only explanation for the disparities we see. Why is it important for the church to be different—a place where we can graciously ask hard questions—as we pursue justice together?

4 C. S. Lewis warns us against clinging to damning explanations and taking pleasure in thinking our enemies are as bad as possible. In today's political climate, that has, sadly, become the norm. Where might you be guilty of this assume-the-worst mindset? If you are comfortable sharing with others, do so. At some point this week, go before the cross of Jesus and ask the Holy Spirit to generate love, peace, and patience in your heart.

5 What can you do this week to apply the truths of this session as you seek to truly execute justice as Scripture commands?

Wrap Up

Have someone read Samuel's story out loud, then answer the closing question.

The parable of talents in Matthew 25 opens with a wealthy man entrusting his property to three servants. The wealthy man entrusted five talents to the first, two to the second, and one talent to the third servant. The first two servants worked hard to make a profit for their master, doubling the money entrusted to them. The second servant didn't receive as much money as the first. Although he also returned a 100-percent profit, he did not equal the first slave's total profit. Despite this disparity, Jesus made it clear that the master was equally pleased with them because both were faithful (Matt. 25:23). The third failed to steward his master's money. He hid it in the ground and accused his master of exploiting others to increase his wealth. He blamed his lack of profit on his master's character, not his own. So the master punished him.

This parable has implications for how we think about disparity. If the first two servants where white and the third was black, would it change your perception of the parable? Keep in mind that the master's and the servants' characters, as Jesus described, would be unchanged. The only new information would be the servants' skin colors.

If we accept the doctrine that racial disparities prove racial discrimination, then we are forced to conclude that the master was racist. But racial disparities are not—on their own—evidence of racial discrimination. Laws that discriminate against people because of their skin color would indeed be evidence of ongoing systemic racism. Slavery and Jim Crow segregation were tragic cases of this. Thankfully, such laws have been abolished in the United States.

As a black man, I understand the temptation to ascribe disparities to discrimination, especially since racism did create vast disparities between black and white Americans through history. But things have changed. While blaming disparities on ongoing *systemic* racism may win us applause, it is no longer true or helpful. The Bible teaches me that I shouldn't compare my blessings with those of my (white) neighbors. It teaches me that accusing people of racism without evidence is slander. It teaches me that if I am faithful over the blessings God gives me, He will bless me further. Disparities are often evidence of differences, not discrimination. God entrusts people with different blessings or privileges—because he values faithfulness, not parity. We're instructed to pursue faithfulness and biblical justice, not parity.

Samuel Sey works at the Canadian Centre for Bio-Ethical Reform and writes extensively about racism from a biblical worldview at www.slowtowrite.com.

Which points from this week's session does Samuel's story help to reinforce and deepen, and how can you live out those insights this week in your pursuit of justice?

Discuss and close the session in prayer.

> If you have the book *Confronting Injustice without Compromising Truth*,
> read chapter 8, "The Color Question" before next week's session.

The Color Question

■ ▪ ▪ ■

Does our vision of social justice promote racial strife?

Word

Let's begin our time together in the Word of God. Open with prayer, then have volunteers read the following four passages aloud:

The soul who sins shall die. The son shall not suffer for the iniquity of the father, nor the father suffer for the iniquity of the son. The righteousness of the righteous shall be upon himself, and the wickedness of the wicked shall be upon himself. (Ezekiel 18:20)

For God so loved the world, that he gave his only Son, that whoever believes in him should not perish but have eternal life. For God did not send his Son into the world to condemn the world, but in order that the world might be saved through him. (John 3:16-17)

From now on, therefore, we regard no one according to the flesh. Even though we once regarded Christ according to the flesh, we regard him thus no longer. Therefore, if anyone is in Christ, he is a new creation. The old has passed away; behold, the new has come. All this is from God, who through Christ reconciled us to himself and gave us the ministry of reconciliation. (2 Corinthians 5:16-18)

After this I looked, and behold, a great multitude that no one could number, from every nation, from all tribes and peoples and languages, standing before the throne and before the Lamb, clothed in white robes, with palm branches in their hands, and crying out with a loud voice, "Salvation belongs to our God who sits on the throne, and to the Lamb!" (Revelation 7:9-10)

Welcome

Race is one of the most combustible topics in the world, particularly (but not exclusively) in the United States. Race is understandably an enduring issue after a quarter millennium of legalized slavery in the US, followed by Jim Crow segregation, lynching, denied voting rights and GI benefits, redlining, and more. Some stalwart Christians took a bold stand for justice. Far too many, however, were complicit when they should have confronted injustice.

Race problems are hardly a closed chapter in human history. Fatal encounters of black citizens with police forces have ignited global outrage, spawning powerful organizations like Black Lives Matter.[1] Books like Robin DiAngelo's *White Fragility* and Ibram X. Kendi's *How to be an Antiracist* have become international bestsellers. Diversity training has swept through the world of business, government, education, and virtually all other American institutions in recent years, including Christian institutions. Professional sports and the entertainment industry have become major outlets for racial activism.

Some hail all of this as progress. Others see the cure of antiracist activism as worse than the disease, perhaps even spreading the disease of racism by dividing everyone into melanin-based tribes. Still others deny that the disease of racism still exists, beyond a few scattered Hitler enthusiasts in the backwoods of the South. In short, we're in a mess. But the Bible offers a hopeful way forward. In this session we will ask whether our vision of social justice promotes racial strife.

Watch

Play session 9, "The Color Question." As you watch, use the outline below to follow along and take notes on key insights.

- **Scripture gives us a more profound way of affirming that black lives matter.** Every black life was fearfully and wonderfully made by God himself, bears the divine image, and is worth enough for the Creator to take on flesh and endure torture, execution, and infinite wrath to redeem.

- **Do police fatalities against black image-bearers prove widespread systemic racism?** According to data collected by the *Washington Post* . . .
  - Between 2016 and 2019, 3,939 image-bearers of God were fatally shot by image-bearing police officers, averaging just under 1,000 deaths per year.
  - Of those deaths, roughly half of those victims were white and a quarter were black.
  - Of those deaths, about 4 percent involved the shooting of an unarmed victim, averaging twenty-five unarmed whites and eighteen unarmed blacks per year.
  - Of those unarmed victims, an average of sixteen whites and eight blacks per year were not fleeing the scene.
  - Of those twenty-four unarmed victims per year who were not fleeing the scene, nearly all of them involved victims physically attacking police officers, usually under the influence of drugs or alcohol.[2]

- **The National Association for the Advancement of Colored People provides some of the following stats on racial disparities in America:**
  - African Americans, according to 2014 data, make up 2.3 million of the 6.8 million Americans in correctional systems, which is 34 percent, despite being only 13.4 percent of the population.
  - African Americans are five times more likely to be incarcerated than white Americans.

- African Americans, despite rates of drug usage similar to those of white Americans, are six times more likely to be incarcerated on drug charges.[3]

- **Three important facts about whether America is systemically white supremacist to its core:**

  1. **According to 2018 data from the US Census Bureau, whites rank sixteenth on the scale of "Median Household Income by Selected Ancestry Groups."[4]** *How can we reconcile the Social Justice B narrative that America remains systemically white supremacist to its core when Indians, Taiwanese, Lebanese, Turkish, Chinese, Iranian, Japanese, Pakistani, Filipino, Indonesian, Syrian, Korean, Ghanian, Nigerian, and Guyanese earn more income on average than whites in the United States?*

  2. **Homes with a married mother and father correspond with higher levels of academic and career success for their children, as well as lower rates of criminality and mental disorder.** The rate of black children born out of wedlock has jumped from 24 percent in 1965 to nearly 70 percent in 2016. (Lest we think this family breakdown is a uniquely black problem, the rate for white children born out of wedlock over the same 50 years has skyrocketed from 4 percent to 28 percent.)[5] Nevertheless a black child today is 250 percent more likely than a white child to be born out of wedlock.[6] *Are we to believe that this heartbreaking reality has nothing to do with many of the sad disparities we see today?*

  3. **Ian Rowe, CEO for a network of black charter schools in New York City, cites a recent study of thriving black men in America.** The study found that the growing class of successful black men "followed the success sequence. They finished their education, got a full-time job, they got married, and then they had children, *in that order*. . . . If a kid grows up in a low-income family and follows those steps, only 6 percent will end up in poverty."[7] That is a hopeful message. In

fact, a 2016 study found that the black poverty rate was 22 percent compared with an 11 percent white poverty rate, while the poverty rate for *married* black couples was lower than the white poverty rate (7.5 percent).[8]

- **Do these facts mute the black voice?**
  - The Smithsonian's National Museum of African American History and Culture opened an online portal entitled "Talking about Race" to help inspire "productive conversation about race."[9] As starting points for the conversation, the Smithsonian offers readers a crash course in three basic terms—*whiteness, white privilege*, and *white fragility.*
  - Liberal white women crafted and popularized all three of these concepts: *whiteness* from Judith Katz, *white privilege* from Peggy McIntosh, and *white fragility* from Robin DiAngelo.
  - Most conversations about race, including those within the church, begin by stipulating that *racism* does not mean discriminating against people on the basis of their race, but rather "prejudice plus power," a redefinition invented by a white sociologist named Patricia Bidol-Padva.[10]

    > Relatively well-off, highly educated, liberal *whites* tend to be among the most zealous in identifying and prosecuting new forms of racism. . . . Whites tend to be more "woke" on racial issues than the average black or Hispanic; they tend to perceive much more racism against minorities than most minorities themselves. . . . Indeed, evidence is growing that many fashionable formulations of "racism" (and antiracist activism) may be directly pernicious for people of color.[11]
    >
    > *—Musa al-Gharbi*

- **Ekemini Uwan on "whiteness as wickedness."**

> When we talk about white identity, then we have to talk about what whiteness is. Well, the reality is that whiteness is rooted in plunder, in theft, in slavery, in enslavement of Africans, genocide of Native Americans. . . . It's a power structure, that is what whiteness is. . . . Because we have to understand something—whiteness is wicked. It is wicked. It's rooted in violence, it's rooted in theft, it's rooted in plunder, it's rooted in power, in privilege.[12]
>
> —*Ekemini Uwan*

- **Three questions about whiteness as wickedness.**

1. Does claiming that "whiteness is wicked" drop a glamor filter over nonwhite cultures (e.g., Idi Amin, Attila the Hun, Pol Pot, Genghis Khan, Pablo Escobar, etc.)? Wickedness is not merely a *white* problem, it is a *human* problem.

> From a narrow perspective, the lesson that some draw from the history of slavery, automatically conceived of as the enslavement of blacks by whites, is that white people were or are uniquely evil. Against the broader background of world history, however, a very different lesson might be that no people of any color can be trusted with unbridled power over any other people, for such power has been grossly abused by whatever race, class, or political authority has held that power. . . . The story of how human beings treat other human beings when they have unbridled power over them is seldom a pretty story or even a decent story, regardless of the color of the people involved.[13]
>
> —*Thomas Sowell*

2. Does claiming that "whiteness is wicked" cherry-pick the most damning aspects of people-with-less-melanin's legacy?

> What was historically unusual [in the West] was the emergence in the late eighteenth century of a strong moral sense that slavery was so wrong that Christians could not in good conscience enslave anyone or countenance the continuation of this institution among themselves or others.[14]
>
> *—Thomas Sowell*

3. Is the definition of whiteness as wickedness unnecessarily inflammatory?

> If I insist on defining "moron" to mean "French hockey player," I shouldn't be surprised if a roomful of French hockey players is offended by my defini- tion! We should choose words that convey our meaning as clearly as possible and—as Christians—as charitably as possible.[15]
>
> *—Neil Shenvi*

• **Closing Scriptures**

Everyone shall die for his own iniquity. (Jeremiah 31:30)

We must all appear before the judgment seat of Christ, so that each one may receive what is due for what he has done in the body, whether good or evil. (2 Corinthians 5:10)

Fathers shall not be put to death because of their children, nor shall children be put to death because of their fathers. Each one shall be put to death for his own sin. (Deuteronomy 24:16)

The soul who sins shall die. The son shall not suffer for the iniquity of the father, nor the father suffer for the iniquity of the son. The righteousness of the righteous shall be upon himself, and the wickedness of the wicked shall be upon himself. (Ezekiel 18:20)

There is therefore now no condemnation for those who are in Christ Jesus. (Romans 8:1).

Wrestle

To better internalize and act on what you just watched, choose three of the five questions below to wrestle through as a group.

1 **Which points from the video session resonated with you most profoundly? Write down the top two or three insights you gained from this session, and briefly share one with the group.**

2 It is an undeniable truth that segments of the church through history have championed or been complicit in vile forms of racism, including slavery, lynching, and segregation. Clarify three to five biblical doctrines that refute the notion that one race is inherently superior to another.

3 How does a biblical worldview enable us as Christians to say "black lives matter" in a manner more profound and expansive than the teachings and philosophies of today's secular movements that bear the Black Lives Matter label? What do we affirm as biblical, and what do we refute as unbiblical and unhelpful?

4 Why are claims such as "whiteness is wicked" and other charges that emerge from critical race theory unhelpful if the church seeks to be an "every tongue, tribe, and nation" witness of the unifying power of the gospel? How might they work against Christian unity?

5 What can you do this week to apply the truths of this session as you seek to truly execute justice as Scripture commands?

Wrap Up

Have someone read Monique's story out loud, then answer the closing question.

At dinner, my pops uttered those five dreaded words: "Let's make America great again." I was shocked! I am adopted. My family is white. I am African American. When has America ever been great for me? "Never trust white people!" was a running theme of my upbringing, and I carried those skin-deep judgments with me everywhere. As a sociology major, I found a label for the framework I had learned growing up. My professors espoused critical race theory (or CRT), which validated my biases, and I spent the next two decades preaching CRT.

My family and I disagreed on issues of systemic racism. One night I prayed, "God, open my family's eyes to their privilege and how people of color live under nonstop oppression in America." The answer to my prayer came as a deep shock. "Monique, you need to repent of your views on social justice." I was convinced the Lord would never say something like that. But he did. And so, I have begun the painful process of untangling my faith from CRT.

The first step in that journey was taking a serious look at the roots of my faith. I discovered the deep conflict between a Christian worldview and CRT. With CRT's constant focus on evil systems, I had become oblivious to the evil and prejudices in my own heart. I wasn't just a victim of America's racist systems; I also perpetuated the racism I claimed to hate.

Salvation is the good news of Jesus's life, death, and resurrection so sinners of all colors can be saved by a free act of divine grace. CRT had pulled me away from that good news into a social justice gospel in which the finished work of Jesus wasn't enough. Scripture consistently defines us as brothers and sisters thanks to Christ. CRT splits us into intersectional tribes. In God's eyes, humanity's fundamental problem is that we are all sinners in need of grace. According to CRT, humanity's fundamental problems are whiteness and oppression. The beliefs of CRT weren't "part of the gospel;" they formed a different gospel altogether.

The Bible is clear: we should not show favoritism or speak evil over each other. But CRT made it nearly impossible to see white people as beloved image-bearers whom Christ died to redeem. This hampered my ability to treat people with the love that Christ has for me. God has a much better way to bring justice and unity than I do. And there's grace for all of us.

Monique Duson serves as founder of the Center for Biblical Unity, which offers resources, training, and videos on racial justice from a biblical perspective at www.centerforbiblicalunity.com.

Which points from this week's session does Monique's story help to reinforce and deepen, and how can you live out those insights this week in your pursuit of justice?

Discuss and close your session in prayer.

If you have the book *Confronting Injustice without Compromising Truth*, read chapter 9, "The Gospel Question," before next week's session.

The Gospel Question

■ ■ ■ ■

Does our vision of social justice distort
the best news in history?

Word

Let's begin our time together in the Word of God. Open with prayer, then have volunteers read the following four passages aloud:

> The Lord is merciful and gracious,
>> slow to anger and abounding in steadfast love.
> He will not always chide,
>> nor will he keep his anger forever.
> He does not deal with us according to our sins,
>> nor repay us according to our iniquities. (Psalm 103:8-10)

> I delivered to you as of first importance what I also received: that Christ died for our sins in accordance with the Scriptures, that he was buried, that he was raised on the third day. (1 Corinthians 15:3-4)

I am astonished that you are so quickly deserting him who called you in the grace of Christ and are turning to a different gospel—not that there is another one, but there are some who trouble you and want to distort the gospel of Christ. (Galatians 1:6-7)

Contend for the faith that was once for all delivered to the saints. (Jude v. 3)

Welcome

NBC airs a hit show called *The Good Place* (a synonym for heaven). A superhuman being named Michael, played by Ted Danson, is befuddled by the fact that, for centuries, no one on earth has accumulated enough good points to avoid eternal anguish in "the bad place." Keep in mind, the theology of the show has no category for salvation by grace. You can make it to "the good place" only by accumulating enough good works. The plot unfolds in an all-law, no-gospel universe. Why has no one been worthy of the good place for centuries? Upon finding that simply buying a tomato counts as negative 12.368 points, Michael finally solves the problem: "It's impossible for anyone to be good enough for the Good Place. . . . These days just buying a tomato at a grocery store means that you are unwittingly supporting toxic pesticides, exploiting labor, contributing to global warming."[1] As condemned character Tahani, played by Jameela Jamil, laments, it "feels like a game you can't win."[2]

In a culture gripped by a Social Justice B mindset, we find ourselves in the same unwinnable game. As Social Justice B educators Özlem Sensoy and Robin DiAngelo put it, we should "work from the knowledge that the societal default is oppression; there are no spaces free from it. Thus, the question becomes, 'How is it manifesting here?' rather than 'Is it manifesting here?'"[3] Do you see how this becomes a game no one can win?

If everything is unjust all the time, then we end up with a bottomless sense of never doing enough, of having more sin than we could possibly atone for. Against this stands the "there is therefore now no condemnation for those who are in Christ Jesus" good news of the Bible. Thanks to Christ's birth, sin-free life, substitutionary death, and bodily resurrection, Jesus is all the perfection we will ever need! This gospel truth does not erase but enhances our drive to do real justice. In this session we will ask whether our vision of social justice distorts the best news in history.

Watch

Play session 10, "The Gospel Question." As you watch, use the outline below to follow along and take notes on key insights.

- **Lewis's first things first principle.**

> Every preference of a small good to a great, or partial good to a total good, involves the loss of the small or partial good for which the sacrifice is made. . . . You can't get second things by putting them first. You get second things only by putting first things first.[4]
>
> —C. S. Lewis

- **What is the "first thing" according to Scripture?** The gospel is *en protois*, a Greek turn of phrase that could be translated "of first importance," "most important," or "of chief significance."

> Now I would remind you, brothers, of the gospel I preached to you. . . . For I delivered to you as *of first importance* what I also received: that Christ died for our sins in accordance with the Scriptures, that he was buried, that he was raised on the third day in accordance with the Scriptures. (1 Corinthians 15:1, 3-4, emphasis added)

- **The gospel is an indicative, not an imperative—good news, not a command.**

- **When we say that doing justice is the gospel or is part of the gospel, then we reduce the good news to an imperative and miss out on the best news in the universe.**

- **We are left with the hopeless gospel of Social Justice B.**

  Infinite responsibility means infinite guilt, a kind of Christianity without salvation: to see power in every interaction is to see sin in every interaction. All that the activist can offer to absolve herself is Sisyphean effort until burnout. Eady's summarization is simpler: "Everything is problematic."[5]

  —Conor Barnes

- **Under the works-based system of Social Justice B, we all become Martin Luthers before he came to understand the good news of God's grace.**

  I am not ashamed of the gospel, for it is the power of God for salvation to everyone who believes. (Romans 1:16)

- **Social Justice B becomes a false means of justification, a way of securing our righteous identity apart from Christ.** But Christ alone is the only ground of our righteous standing.

The kind of moral outrage we typically classify as altruistic is often a function of self-interest, wielded to assuage feelings of personal culpability for societal harms or reinforce (to the self and others) one's own status as a Very Good Person.[6]

−Elizabeth Nolan Brown

- **What about Luke 4?** Doesn't this passage make social justice an essential ingredient of the gospel?

> The Spirit of the Lord is upon me,
>> because He has anointed me
>> to proclaim good news to the poor.
> He has sent me to proclaim liberty to the captives,
>> and recovering of sight to the blind,
>> to set at liberty those who are oppressed,
> to proclaim the year of the Lord's favor. (Luke 4:18-19)

- **Five questions about Luke 4.**

1. Is it important to avoid reading our personal politics and perspectives into Scripture?

2. Is it possible to take this passage—Jesus's words in Luke 4—out of context in a way that hurts the poor and oppressed?

3. If Luke 4 means that the gospel is about confronting social injustice, then what social injustices did Jesus confront that day?

4. What does Jesus actually preach to the poor?
   - Knowing the *audience* is different from knowing the *announcement* itself. Luke 4 speaks to the audience, namely, the poor.
   - "Jesus came into Galilee, proclaiming the gospel of God, and saying, 'The time is fulfilled, and the kingdom of God is at hand; repent and believe in the gospel'" (Mark 1:14–15).
   - Two verses later Jesus calls his first disciples with the invitation, "Follow me." To become a disciple of a rabbi was a long and arduous task. Candidates for discipleship often had to shadow rabbis for years, proving their merit and moral fitness. If they proved themselves worthy, they would hear the rabbi utter, "Follow me." Jesus launches his entire ministry with an act of grace that spoke those cherished words to men who had done nothing to prove themselves.
   - His disciples are shocked and ask, "'Then who can be saved?' Jesus looked at them and said, 'With man it is impossible, but not with God. For all things are possible with God'" (Mark 10:26–27).
   - Jesus says his mission on earth is to "give his life as a ransom for many" (Mark 10:45).

- After his resurrection, Jesus commands his disciples to "go into all the world and proclaim the gospel to the whole creation. Whoever believes and is baptized will be saved, but whoever does not believe will be condemned" (Mark 16:15–16).
- In Luke we find the famous parable of the prodigal son, in which Jesus makes it clear that God runs to us, embraces us, and showers us with blessings as a divine act of free, ill-deserved grace.
- In Luke 18:13–14, it is not the Pharisee flaunting his own righteousness and giving to the poor, but the tax collector beating his breast, crying, "God, be merciful to me, a sinner!" who goes home justified before God.
- At the first Lord's Supper, Jesus speaks of his death, saying, "This cup that is poured out for you is the new covenant in my blood" (Luke 22:20).
- Later Jesus tells the poor thief on the cross, "Truly, I say to you, today you will be with me in paradise" (Luke 23:43), though the thief had no time before his final breath to do any good works.
- In the book of John, Jesus addresses the poor on the shores of Capernaum. The crowd asks, "What must we do, to be doing the works of God?" (John 6:28). Jesus did not say, "Go reform unjust systems." Instead, "Jesus answered them, 'This is the work of God, that you believe in him whom he has sent'" (John 6:29).
- At Lazarus's tomb Jesus declares, "I am the resurrection and the life. Whoever believes in me, though he die, yet shall he live, and everyone who lives and believes in me shall never die" (John 11:25–26).
- In sum, there is no shortage of red letters to help us discern what Jesus actually preached to the poor. Salvation by God's grace alone through Christ is good news for the poor because it definitively refutes the oppressors' message that their lives have no value.

5. Is it possible that redefining "the gospel" to include our own visions of social justice can prove harmful (e.g., Salvador Allende's Chile)? Instead of misinterpreting Luke 4 as a proof text for our highly fallible political ideologies, let us "contend for the faith that was once for all delivered to the saints" (Jude v. 3).

Wrestle

To better internalize and act on what you just watched, choose three of the five questions below to wrestle through as a group.

1 Which points from the video session resonated with you most profoundly? Write down the top two or three insights you gained from this session, and briefly share one with the group.

2 Paul teaches that the gospel of God's saving grace through the death and resurrection of Jesus is "of first importance" and warns us with stern and passionate language against those who preach false gospels that seek to add human works to God's grace. In what ways might social justice become a false gospel?

3 Why is it important to clarify that justice flows from the gospel but is not identical to or part of the gospel itself? What is at stake in how we define justice and its relationship to the gospel?

4 What does it mean to keep the gospel as our first thing? What habits can we form to keep the gospel first in our daily lives? How can participation in a local church, taking the sacraments, investing in our prayer lives, and preaching the gospel to ourselves and others keep us from turning "the gospel first" into an empty slogan?

5 What can you do this week to apply the truths of this session as you seek to truly execute justice as Scripture commands?

Wrap Up

Have someone read Ojo's story out loud, then answer the closing question.

Social justice is all the rage these days. On one level, it is a welcome change that people seem to care more about justice. Yet the more I engage in social justice discussions with fellow millennials or gen Zers, the more disheartened I become. With this surge in social justice discourse there has been a steady increase in cynicism, and in some cases downright hatred toward people who are guilty of thinking about things in the "wrong way." The scary thing is that this is not happening just in the secular world but also within much of the church.

This reality has hit close to home for me over the past couple of years. Friends in my inner circle have been strong Bible-believing Christians. They have heard Scripture's call for justice, a call that has sadly been ignored in certain segments of the church. Their perception of the church's silence on matters of injustice such as explicit racism has sent a loud and clear message that the church can't be trusted in matters of justice. Slowly but surely, young Christians begin looking outside the church and to the world for solutions to combat the injustice they see. When churches fail to live out biblical justice in a beautiful and compelling way, they turn rising generations into easy prey for social justice ideologues.

The results have been tragic. Biblical morality is slowly replaced with the evolving moralism of progressive politics. Soon the Bible itself is deconstructed as an oppressive tool of the cisheteropatriarchy instead of the life-giving words of a loving Creator. Truth is eventually seen as relative and socially constructed as opposed to defined by God. The uniqueness of Christ's saving work is abandoned. What started as a noble pursuit of justice becomes an erosion of a biblical worldview, and the gospel is lost.

Some of my friends realized the fatal compromises being made in the name of social justice and woke up. But others have become nominally Christian or in some cases no longer identify as Christians. My heart breaks for them, and I pray that they find their way back to the Lord. More than ever, I pray for revival and for the church to recommit itself to being a beacon to the watching world of what it means to act justly. To do that without succumbing to the ideologies of our age, we must make our highest priority what Scripture itself ranks "of first importance"—the gospel of the death and resurrection of Jesus.

Ojo Ojoye has worked at Arizona State University and is currently training for lifelong ministry.

Which points from this week's session does Ojo's story help to reinforce and deepen, and how can you live out those insights this week in your pursuit of justice?

Discuss and close your session in prayer.

Suggested Prayer to Redeem Sinners and Systems

God,

You are so holy and so committed to redemption that you oppose all sin—our individual sins as well as those we embed in systems whenever we "frame injustice by statute." Mark our hearts with that same commitment. As we seek to bring redemption to fallen systems, may we not fall into the traps of automatically assuming the most damning explanations for inequalities, ignoring evidence that may not support our ideologies, or telling self-serving narratives that pin all oppression on this or that people group. And most of all, make your first thing our first thing. The good news of Jesus's death and resurrection is "of first importance" according to your Word. Help us contend earnestly for the gospel and not try to add anything to the complete and sufficient saving work of Jesus. It would be easy to say we believe that gospel and then sit on our thumbs while people suffer. So please push us to do the kind of justice you command, the justice that is not the gospel itself but flows beautifully from that gospel. Amen.

If you have the book *Confronting Injustice without Compromising Truth*, read chapter 10, "The Tunnel Vision Question," before next week's session.

The Tunnel Vision Question

■ ■ ■ ■

Does our vision of social justice make one way of seeing
something the only way of seeing everything?

Word

Let's begin our time together in the Word of God. Open with prayer, then have volunteers
read the following four passages aloud:

Love the Lord your God . . . with all your mind. (Matthew 22:37)

It is my prayer that your love may abound more and more, with knowledge and all
discernment. (Philippians 1:9)

He shall not judge by what his eyes see,
    or decide disputes by what his ears hear,
but with righteousness he shall judge the poor,
    and decide with equity for the meek of the earth.
        (Isaiah 11:3-4, speaking of Jesus)

Test everything; hold fast what is good. Abstain from every form of evil. (1 Thessalonians
5:21-22)

Welcome

Every mind has what philosophers would call an "epistemology," what programmers might call an "operating system." How should we best process and store the input and data of life? Should we feel, reason, experiment, trust, revolt, or Google our way to truth?

These aren't questions for pipe-puffing philosophers in rich mahogany offices with many leather-bound books. Everyone has an epistemology, and, as with computer operating systems, some are better than others. Some mental operating systems open our minds to new truths, while others are so riddled with bugs and viruses that they generate jumbled beliefs and crash cognitive systems.

If our mental operating systems are buggy, loving God and loving our neighbors will be difficult. If, for example, I seek truth at the psychic's shop—if palm readings, tarot cards, and Ouija boards are where I stake my trust—then my mind will not blossom into all that God designed it to be. My God-given capacities to know him deeply, reason well, weigh evidence, trust what is trustworthy, and see through propaganda—all of that God-given, intellectual potential will be squandered.

Again, the Bible does not merely say "do justice" but to "truly execute justice." Corrupted mental operating systems generate false beliefs that can easily dupe us into thinking we are doing great work for others, when in reality we are doing them damage. If we care about justice—giving both God and others what is due them—then we should care about epistemology. In this session we will pinpoint one of the primary ways epistemologies go wrong, asking whether our vision of social justice makes one way of seeing something the only way of seeing everything.

Watch

Play session 11, "The Tunnel Vision Question." As you watch, use the outline below to follow along and take notes on key insights.

- **Tribes thinking is the trendy epistemology of our day.** Within the Social Justice B epistemology, the story of oppression is typically told in one of six ways:

T, beware the **T**heocrats!

The oppressors are right-wing Christians trying to cram their outdated morality down everyone else's throats with the coercive powers of law.

R, beware the **R**acists!

The oppressors are those who marginalize and dehumanize people who don't share their skin tone or ethnic identity.

I, beware the **I**slamophobes!

The oppressors are those who fear that most if not all Muslims are hate-mongering terrorists rather than peace-loving neighbors.

B, beware the **B**igots!

The oppressors are those who use their heteronormative power to deny the rights and humanity of the LGBTQ community.

E, beware the **E**xploiters!

The oppressors are those whose capitalist greed leads them to use and abuse the poor for their own selfish, materialistic gain.

S, beware the **S**exists!

The oppressors are men who deny equal rights, equal access to power, and equal pay to maintain a patriarchal tyranny over half our species.

- **Some epistemologies, or approaches to knowledge, give us tunnel vision, taking one insight into some of reality and making it the only way to interpret all of reality.**

- **Seeing what is not there.** Do factors other than sexism contribute to the gender pay gap? Tribes thinking will not allow us to even explore the question. It makes us close-minded and causes concept creep.

- **In addition to causing us to often see things that are not there, Tribes thinking causes us to miss real forms of oppression that are there.** Here are six examples:

  1. We should care for women exploited by the abortion industry.

     Facts for justice-seekers:
     - Of women who seek abortions, 64 percent said they felt pressured by others and over half thought abortion was "morally wrong."[1]
     - Less than 1 percent said they felt better about themselves, 77.9 percent felt guilt, and 59.5 percent felt that "part of me died."[2]
     - Women who have had abortions face an 81 percent increased risk of mental health problems.[3] Does our vision of social justice include these women or take their harrowing stories seriously?[4]

  2. We should care for the voiceless babies terminated by the abortion industry.

     Facts for justice-seekers:
     - Abortion was the leading cause of death worldwide in 2018, tallying 42 million victims.[5] That is eighty image-bearers terminated in the last minute, more than one per second.
     - In places such as Iceland, "the abortion rate for children diagnosed with Down syndrome approaches 100 percent,"[6] while in the United States, 90 percent of preborn humans diagnosed with Downs are terminated.[7]

- In Asia, widespread sex-selective abortions have led to as many as 160 million "missing" women—more than the entire female population of the United States. Recent evidence suggests that sex-selective abortions of girls are common among certain populations in the United States as well.[8]
- In cities such as New York, more black babies are aborted than are born.[9]

3. We should care about children who have endured split homes.

   Facts for justice-seekers:
   - There are mountains of research documenting the advantages of being raised by two parents. Mom and Dad sticking together, for all their imperfections, corresponds with higher levels of academic and career success for their children, along with lower rates of criminality and mental disorder.
   - One of the world's most popular Social Justice B organizations publicly declared its "guiding principle" to "disrupt the Western-prescribed nuclear family" in its mission statement.[10]
   - Black children born to unmarried mothers climbed from 25 to a heartbreaking 70 percent from 1965 to 2017. White children born out of wedlock skyrocketed from 4 to over 28 percent over the same period.[11]

4. We should care about the victims of the exploitative pornography industry.

   Facts for justice-seekers:
   - Pornography is a $97 billion industry.[12] In 2018 more than 5.5 billion hours of pornography were consumed on a single porn site, with 33.5 billion visits.[13]
   - According to the Internet Watch Foundation, recorded child sexual exploitation (otherwise known as "child porn") is one of the fastest-growing online businesses, with over 624,000 child porn traders discovered in the US.[14]
   - Analysis of the fifty most popular pornographic videos found that 88 percent of scenes contained physical violence.
   - Then there are the established links between pornography and human trafficking, rape, domestic violence, impaired brain function, broken relationships, and depression.[15]

5. We should care about the millions of Christians imprisoned or executed around the globe.

   Facts for justice-seekers:
   - According to *Newsweek* in 2018, "Christian persecution and genocide is worse now than 'any time in history.'"[16] This includes being targeted, imprisoned, beaten, raped, hung, crucified, and bombed for claiming Jesus as Lord.
   - Every month an average of 345 Christians are killed for faith-related reasons, 105 churches or Christian buildings are burned or attacked, and 219 Christians are detained without trial.[17]

6. We should care about the desperately oppressed victims of far-left systems like communism and socialism.

   Facts for justice-seekers:
   - According to the international bestseller *The Black Book of Communism*, the quest to achieve economic equality between the rich and poor through communist and socialist policies has resulted in over one hundred million casualties in the twentieth century alone.[18]
   - Support for socialism is trending high in the United States, particularly among younger generations. These are the same generations in which one-third believe that more people perished under George W. Bush than Joseph Stalin, and almost half are "unfamiliar" with Mao Zedong and the fifty million victims of his plan for economic equality.[19]
   - If social justice is truly about ending oppression, why are many Social Justice B advocates quick to fall for the lofty rhetoric of "compassionate" political visions that led to the oppression and termination of more people in the last century than any other system?

- **The tunnel vision of Tribes thinking misses the main thing—the gospel as liberation from the oppression of the world, the flesh, and the devil.**

Wrestle

To better internalize and act on what you just watched, choose three of the five questions below to wrestle through as a group.

1 Which points from the video session resonated with you most profoundly? Write down the top two or three insights you gained from this session, and briefly share one with the group.

2 Which kernels of truth in Tribes thinking should Christians take seriously and affirm?

3 What are three ways Tribes thinking conflicts with a biblical worldview? How might you winsomely explain those conflicts to a brother or sister in Christ who may have embraced Social Justice B?

4 This session covered several injustices, including abortion, broken homes, pornography, Christian persecution, and socialist repression. Which of these issues stirs the deepest sense of injustice within you and why?

5 What can you do this week to apply the truths of this session as you seek to truly execute justice as Scripture commands?

Wrap Up

Have someone read Neil's story out loud, then answer the closing question.

I became a Christian in graduate school at UC Berkeley while obtaining a PhD in theoretical chemistry. Because I wanted to reach my fellow academics with the gospel, I plunged headlong into the world of apologetics. I tried to avoid "political issues," believing that Christians should center their faith on the life, death, and resurrection of Jesus and the authority of Scripture.

A few years ago, I noticed a theological drift in certain Christians, often beginning with an interest in "social justice." Many moved from conservative denominations to progressive ones and sometimes left the Christian faith altogether. Why? I began reading voraciously and discovered that contemporary "Social Justice B" is rooted in a comprehensive ideology that emerged from a discipline known as "critical theory," which divides people between oppressed groups and oppressor groups along lines of race, class, gender, sexuality, physical ability, and age. Because of their "social location," oppressors are blinded by their privilege, while oppressed people have special insight into social reality.

This framework has devastating effects on our theology. First, a Christian's primary identity is in their union with Christ. To see our brothers and sisters as "oppressors" solely because of their demographic group is to re-erect the dividing wall of hostility that Christ tore down (Eph. 2:14). Second, while unbiblical values oppress, God's values are ultimately liberating. We dare not haphazardly dismantle all society's values, but ask which values are consistent with Scripture. Third, our ultimate authority must always be God's voice in Scripture. Someone's membership of a marginalized group does not make them an infallible interpreter of reality. Finally, our primary problem is sin, and the solution is God reaching into history through the work of Jesus to rescue us from our rebellion and restore us to himself.

Many are adopting a comprehensive framework that inevitably unravels basic Christian doctrines. Don't just coast along with the cultural zeitgeist. Test all things. Think critically and think biblically.

Neil Shenvi is a PhD in theoretical chemistry from UC Berkeley who researches and writes extensively about social justice and critical theory from a Christian worldview perspective at www.shenviapologetics.com.

Which points from this week's session does Neil's story help to reinforce and deepen, and how can you live out those insights this week in your pursuit of justice? Discuss and close your session in prayer.

> If you have the book *Confronting Injustice without Compromising Truth*, read chapter 11, "The Suffering Question," before next week's session.

The Suffering Question

■ ■ ■ ■

Does our vision of social justice turn the "lived experience" of hurting people into more pain?

Word

Let's begin our time together in the Word of God. Open with prayer, then have volunteers read the following four passages aloud:

> Know this, my beloved brothers: let every person be quick to hear, slow to speak, slow to anger. (James 1:19)

> Bless those who persecute you; bless and do not curse them. Rejoice with those who rejoice, weep with those who weep. (Romans 12:14-15)

> For God gave us a spirit not of fear but of power and love and self-control. (2 Timothy 1:7)

> Fear not, for I am with you;
>> be not dismayed, for I am your God;
> I will strengthen you, I will help you,
>> I will uphold you with my righteous right hand. (Isaiah 41:10)

Welcome

Since I'm a speck on a blue dot in a gigantic universe, my perspective is often *way* off. I leap to wrong conclusions. I make snap judgments about other people and their motives. I can take my own experiences and my own interpretation of those experiences as far more authoritative than they actually are.

That is one reason the Bible is so important to me. It keeps me from taking my own conclusions and feelings too seriously. It is a two-thousand-page reminder that I am not the final word on reality. I am, indeed, a speck on a blue dot. That's why I try to take the words of the One who made this speck and this blue dot more seriously than I take myself.

This realization brings us to a second aspect of Tribes thinking. It encourages us to make our own "lived experiences" authoritative, a view known as "standpoint epistemology." When applied to questions of justice, this means that anyone who claims that theocrats, racists, Islamophobes, bigots, exploiters, or sexists have hurt them must not be merely heard but taken authoritatively. Lived experiences must, in turn, become the foundations on which we rebuild everything from public policy and school curriculum to theological systems and church ministry. Questioning the narratives of the oppressed and the policies or theologies derived from them makes *you* the oppressor. This is a mark of Social Justice B. But does elevating certain perspectives to unquestionable status help us love the oppressed as Scripture commands? In this session we will ask whether our vision of social justice turns the "lived experience" of hurting people into more pain.

Watch

Play session 12, "The Suffering Question." As you watch, use the outline below to follow along and take notes on key insights.

- **The Bible commands us to "be quick to hear" (James 1:19), "bear one another's burdens" (Galatians 6:2), and "weep with those who weep" (Romans 12:15).** Consider the story of hip-hop artist Shai Linne:

This is about how being a black man in America has shaped both the way I see myself and the way others have seen me my whole life. . . . It's about being hand-cuffed and thrown into the back of a police car while walking down the street during college, and then waiting for a white couple to come identify whether or not I was the one who'd committed a crime against them, knowing that if they said I was the one, I would be immediately taken to jail, no questions asked. . . . It's about the exhaustion of constantly feeling I have to assert my humanity in front of some white people I'm meeting for the first time, to let them know, "Hey! I'm not a threat! You don't need to be afraid. If you got to know me, I'm sure we have things in common!" . . . It's about having to explain to my 4-year-old son at his mostly white Christian school that the kids who laughed at him for having brown skin were wrong, that God made him in his image, and that his skin is beautiful—after he told me, "Daddy, I don't want brown skin. I want white skin."[1]

—Shai Linne

- **Biblical listening is different than Social Justice B and Tribes thinking's emphasis on "lived experiences."**

- **Tribes thinking ignites the uh-oh center of people's brain by generalizing their trauma.** This is the opposite of what good psychologists do with rational cognitive therapy and exposure therapy. In short, Tribes thinking is cruel.

- **The Bible is as anti-fear as it is anti-oppression.** God commands us to "fear not" over a hundred times. If we advance ideologies that generalize people's painful experiences, leave them chronically triggered, and set their uh-oh centers ablaze, then we should not pretend that we are doing the kind of justice Scripture commands.

- **When it comes to doing justice, reality matters.** Tribes thinking, however, forces us to take our "lived experience" as the final word on reality itself, forbidding us from fact-checking our feelings.

Wrestle

To better internalize and act on what you just watched, choose three of the five questions below to wrestle through as a group.

1 Which points from the video session resonated with you most profoundly? Write down the top two or three insights you gained from this session, and briefly share one with the group.

2 Lived experiences matter. Writing off people's stories is easy if we immediately associate them with political ideologies we disagree with. How can we resist this urge and be more present with people in their pain? How can we bring the gospel to bear on their pain?

3 God commands us to be fearless. In what ways can we end up inadvertently making people more fearful and easily triggered in the name of "social justice"?

4 Why is the pursuit of truth essential to the biblical pursuit of justice, and how does Tribes thinking derail us in that pursuit? How can serious thinking and research, even if our conclusions go against the political orthodoxies of our day, make us more effective in loving the oppressed?

5 What can you do this week to apply the truths of this session as you seek to truly execute justice as Scripture commands?

Wrap Up

Have someone read Bella's story out loud, then answer the closing question.

I chased the mirage of love in fraternity houses and the beds of strangers. It left me aching. I made friends who had a "solution" to my pain: fighting injustice with anger. I learned that men are predators, religion is oppressive, and "morality" is only a construct. What I didn't know is that when you choose an anger-fueled life, you choose a fear-controlled life. Scariest of all, I didn't know where to find my self-worth. After two years of living this way, I needed to recalibrate and took a year off from school.

I took an internship with an anti-sex-trafficking organization in Germany. I wanted to be enough to save these women but was no match for this evil—women sold for consumption and pimps using sex as a weapon. Absolute evil really did exist, and I was looking at it. In that troubled stillness, I heard a whisper. It said this darkness wasn't the end of the story, that without a good God, this would be all there was, but God cannot be deleted. Jesus and his promises to heal this dark world finally made sense. On a cold spring morning, I cried out to him. God released me from anger and fear. Years of shame slid off me and I was made whole.

I transferred to a Christian university to pursue God. A week after moving, I went dancing in LA with my new roommates. A group of young men drugged me and gang-raped me until five in the morning. When I woke up, there was no denying the black bruises covering my body. I told my roommate, who sobbed with me and went with me to the police station.

As we drove to the station, I expected to feel hopeless and lost. Instead, I felt perfect peace. My Father was holding me in his arms, and I could feel it. I can't put into words how deeply I understood his love that day. I am his precious, beloved daughter; no evil could ever change that. The final chapter of my story is already written and waits for me; it ends with me running into the Father's open arms. No power of hell or scheme of man could pluck me from his hand.

I do not hate anyone, not even my rapists. Jesus paid my full debt on the cross, and anyone who turns to Jesus has theirs paid too. I still care deeply about justice for victims of sexual violence, now more than ever. I draw on God's perfect love for restoration.

Fear can't drive out fear, nor hate drive out hate, only love can do that. And God's love can and will heal the pains of this world a thousand times over, just as it healed mine.

Bella Danusiar is a graduate Biola University student currently training for lifelong gospel ministry and justice work.

Which points from this week's session does Bella's story help to reinforce and deepen, and how can you live out those insights this week in your pursuit of justice? Discuss and close your session in prayer.

> **If you have the book** *Confronting Injustice without Compromising Truth*, **read chapter 12, "The Standpoint Question" before next week's session.**

The Standpoint Question

■　■　■　■

Does our vision of social justice turn the
quest for truth into an identity game?

Word

Let's begin our time together in the Word of God. Open with prayer, then have volunteers read the following four passages aloud:

Hear the cases between your brothers, and judge righteously between a man and his brother or the alien who is with him. You shall not be partial in judgment. You shall hear the small and the great alike. You shall not be intimidated by anyone, for the judgment is God's. (Deuteronomy 1:16-17)

Whoever oppresses a poor man insults his Maker. (Proverbs 14:31)

Whoever is generous to the poor lends to the Lord. (Proverbs 19:17)

Do not judge by appearances, but judge with right judgment. (John 7:24)

Welcome

If you tried to talk about your Christian faith with people in the Western world, say, three hundred years ago, you could trust that most of your conversation partners would share a similar set of presuppositions about the world. Most would believe that God created the universe, that God has revealed himself to humanity, and that obeying God is an integral part of living the good life. Sixty years ago, under the sway of modernism, ideas were typically criticized in the West if they lacked evidence. Ten to twenty years ago, as postmodernism broke mainstream, ideas were criticized not so much because they lacked evidence but because they lacked "tolerance." If a view claimed to be *the* truth instead of *a* truth, it was dismissed as intolerant. Today, as we have entered what I have called the "post-postmodern" era,[1] it is not a lack of evidence or a lack of tolerance but a lack of melanin or a lack of a second X chromosome that makes someone's ideas wrong.

If we don't understand this trendy shift to an epistemology that weighs ideas based on skin tone, gender, and economic status, then connecting with our friends and neighbors under the sway of Social Justice B will be a challenge. This session asks whether our vision of social justice turns the quest for truth into an identity game.

Watch

Play session 13, "The Standpoint Question." As you watch, use the outline below to follow along and take notes on key insights.

- **Unfalsifiability:** When no amount of evidence, facts, or Scripture can contradict our entrenched beliefs.

- **Good worldviews, like Christianity, are falsifiable (1 Corinthians 15).**

- **The Tribes thinking of Social Justice B is unfalsifiable, shielding itself from any meaningful contrary evidence.**

  > Objective, rational, linear thinking [is a mark of] "whiteness." . . . The idea that objectivity is best reached only through rational thought is a specifically Western and masculine way of thinking.[2]
  >
  > —*Margaret L. Andersen and Patricia Hill Collins*

  > Accept the grievances of faculty of color *without question*.[3]
  >
  > —*Tyler Tsay*

  > We are inflicting harm asking for evidence . . . to ask for evidence of racism is racism with a capital R.[4]
  >
  > —*Naima Lowe*

- **Tribes thinking shifts our focus from "isms" to "ists," from ideas to people, from evidence to people's external identity markers.** All we have to do is memorize a handful of condemning buzzwords—white fragility, white privilege, male privilege, toxic masculinity, internalized racism, epistemic exploitation—and at no point do we have to do the hard work of engaging any evidence that contradicts our worldview.

- **Tribes thinking processes ideas as true or false based purely on *melanin* rather than *merit*, *private parts* over *persuasiveness*, and *economic status* over *evidential substance*.** But *ideas* don't have melanin, private parts, or bank accounts, *people* do.

- **Jesus used logic and evidence.**

- **Logic and evidence aren't "white." Millions of image-bearers of all shades and stripes have used their God-given intellects to make the world a better place.**

- **The arguments of this study could be stated by someone who does not share the author's demographic.** That wouldn't magically make them true or false. Writing off someone's viewpoint because of their melanin levels or gender or economic status makes us actual racists, sexists, and bigots.

  > If there is one brutal fact that centuries of white oppression have taught blacks, it
  > is that whites are incapable of making any valid judgments about human existence.[5]
  > −James Cone

- **If old white guys represent an oppressive patriarchy we must abolish, we should ask the following questions:**

  Why does much of Social Justice B doctrine sound so close to the economic theories of Marx, Engels, or Bernie Sanders?

  Why does it advance Rousseau's vision that institutions, not fallen human hearts, are the source of evil?

Why does it often defend the abortion ruling of seven powerful robed men, embrace the expressive sexual ethics crafted by Herbert Marcuse and Wilhelm Reich, espouse an oppressor versus oppressed narrative championed by Antonio Gramsci and the all-white male Frankfurt school, employ the deconstructionist tactics invented by Foucault and Derrida, and practice the political tactics of Saul Alinsky?

These architects of Tribes thinking share something fascinating: they were well-off white guys.[6]

- **Throughout Scripture we find God's special concern for the poor.**
    - God is in such deep solidarity with those in the pains of poverty that Proverbs says, "Whoever oppresses a poor man insults his Maker" (14:31) and, "Whoever is generous to the poor lends to the Lord" (19:17).
    - God speaks judgment against those who cheat the poor (Psalm 140:12; Hosea 12:7).
    - God's law mandates special protections for widows and orphans (Exodus 22:22–23), and the essence of true religion, according to Scripture, is "to visit orphans and widows in their affliction" (James 1:27).

> God's love for justice is grounded in his love for the victims of injustice. And his love for the victims of injustice belongs to his love for the little ones of the world: for the weak, the defenseless, the ones at the bottom, the excluded ones, the miscasts, the outcasts, the outsiders.[7]
>
> –Nicholas Wolterstorff

- **God's solidarity with the poor and oppressed never means that he elevates their perspective to sacred, unquestionable status.**
  - The "all" of "all have sinned and fall short of the glory of God" (Romans 3:23) includes rich, poor, privileged, underprivileged, haves, and have-nots.
  - The oppressed in Egypt were hardly infallible. They bowed to the golden calf (Exodus 32).
  - The paralyzed man in Luke 5:20 was far from rich. Jesus said, "Man, your sins are forgiven."
  - God is "not wishing that any should perish, but that all should reach repentance" (2 Peter 3:9). "Any" and "all" includes the oppressed. We all need repentance.
  - God does not suggest but commands that we not "be partial to a poor man in his lawsuit" (Exodus 23:3).
  - Scripture puts strong standards of evidence for accusations of injustice (Deuteronomy 19:1–2; 1 Timothy 5:19).

- **We are all sinners, rich and poor, in dire need of God's saving grace.**

Wrestle

To better internalize and act on what you just watched, choose three of the five questions below to wrestle through as a group.

1 Which points from the video session resonated with you most profoundly? Write down the top two or three insights you gained from this session, and briefly share one with the group.

2 God commands us to grieve with those who grieve, and feeling someone else's grief is impossible if we don't listen well to their pain. What steps can we take as Christians to be better listeners?

3 Scripture commands us to "truly execute justice," which implies that there are ways to execute justice that we think are helpful but are actually hurtful. Why is weighing ideas based on their merit rather than melanin, their credibility over chromosomes, and their scriptural fidelity over social status important to doing true justice?

4 According to Scripture, God exhibits deep solidarity with the poor and commands us to care for them. What are three habits we can form to help us live these Scriptures well?

5 What can you do this week to apply the truths of this session as you seek to truly execute justice as Scripture commands?

Wrap Up

Have someone read Freddy's story out loud, then answer the closing question.

I was born in rural Appalachia with flickering electricity and no running water. I've heard people say, "We grew up poor, but we never knew it." Well, *we knew it*. Raised by our single mom, my brother and I were "half-breeds," or so we were told. I honestly didn't know what I was—except *different*. In the rugged mountains of Tennessee, my twin and I were the only people of color. We scored the social-pariah trifecta: poor, fatherless, and dark-skinned. Piercing stares and racial pejoratives became my daily experience.

In my early teens, I met Christ. A divorced white lady reached out to disciple me two hours a week, for two years. A young white minister discipled me, then later, an older white pastor. Then, in my duress, a wealthy white church member provided me with much-needed clothes. Generous white widows in the church helped me pay for Christian summer camp.

Ultimately, God called me to ministry. I ended up going to a Christian university known for its fundamentalism. I didn't receive anything resembling equal opportunity perks. I was given dignity, community, and accountability. These imparted me self-respect that was earned. God has been faithful. I became the first in my family to go to college. I have served for two decades in pastoral ministry. I have earned a PhD and serve as the dean of a graduate theological seminary. Best of all, I have an intimate, personal walk with Jesus.

Over the years, I've pieced together the fact that those who wounded me were not racists and bigots *because they were white*; they were racists and bigots who *happened to be white*. I've learned that identity must be based in Christ, not rooted in ethnicity, heritage, or culture. Sadly, because of the direction of culture under the sway of Social Justice B, I've had several ironic experiences. Although a minority who has encountered unmitigated racism in the past, I have become a pariah in many circles. Why? Because I reject today's trending justice ideologies. The intensity of attacks on people who reject identity-based tribalism has become a spiritual pathology in many Christian institutions. But biblical justice exposes today's social justice as a resounding gong or clanging cymbal. Lord, give us the courage to stand for your justice against its counterfeits, no matter the threats to our livelihoods. You are worth it!

Freddy Cardoza serves as dean of Grace Theological Seminary, writes extensively, and hosts multiple podcasts at www.freddycardoza.com.

Which points from this week's session does Freddy's story help to reinforce and deepen, and how can you live out those insights this week in your pursuit of justice? Discuss and close your session in prayer.

Suggested Prayer to Pursue
Truth over Tribes Thinking

God,

You command us to love you with our minds. You are the God of both justice and truth, and you call us to seek both together. When we replace the pursuit of truth with extrabiblical epistemologies, we begin seeing oppression in places where it isn't and overlooking it in places where it is. We push fear-inspiring narratives that inflict pain on those already aching. We assess ideas more on melanin than merit, project the worst motives onto those who disagree with us, and ignore evidence that contradicts our ideologies. We grant people's lived experiences an authority that belongs only to you and your Word. Help us be more like Jesus, who does "not judge by what his eyes see, or decide disputes by what his ears hear, but with righteousness he shall judge the poor, and decide with equity for the meek of the earth." Sharpen our minds to obey Christ's command to "not judge by appearances, but judge with right judgment." Match our justice-seeking with truth-seeking, that we may better reflect who you are to the watching world and more truly execute justice. Amen.

If you have the book *Confronting Injustice without Compromising Truth*, read chapter 13, "Conclusion," before next week's session, and feel free to explore the appendixes for deeper insights.

Conclusion

■ ■ ■ ■

Word

Let's begin our time together in the Word of God. Open with prayer, then have volunteers read the following four passages aloud:

Have no other gods before me. (Exodus 20:3)

Walk in a manner worthy of the calling to which you have been called, with all humility and gentleness, with patience, bearing with one another in love, eager to maintain the unity of the Spirit in the bond of peace. There is one body and one Spirit—just as you were called to the one hope that belongs to your call—one Lord, one faith, one baptism, one God and Father of all, who is over all and through all and in all. (Ephesians 4:1-6)

If we confess our sins, he is faithful and just to forgive us our sins and to cleanse us from all unrighteousness. (1 John 1:9)

Do not judge by appearances, but judge with right judgment. (John 7:24)

Welcome

Welcome to our final session of the *Confronting Injustice without Compromising Truth Video Study*. You made it! Now that we have asked our twelve questions, it should be clear that Social Justice B and Social Justice A are not two different political persuasions, they are two fundamentally different religions. Yes, both are concerned about the oppressed, but in very different ways.

A word of advice: When we hear someone express concern about the way blacks or women are treated, we must be especially careful not to immediately lump them into the Social Justice B category. As I have repeated throughout this series, there is real, sinful racism and sexism in the world. Assuming that a brother or sister who draws our attention to such injustice is automatically a Social Justice B advocate is hardly a way to advance church unity or true justice in the world.

Then there are some Christians who embrace perhaps one or two of the Social Justice B doctrines mentioned. We must also be careful not to project the entire system onto our brothers and sisters who may be wavering on a few points. That would not be helpful. There is, however, a predictable pattern: belief in one Social Justice B doctrine tends to lead to another, then another, until many Christians end up abandoning their faith. I have watched this process play out more times than I care to recall. With love as our motive, rather than the desire to win a political battle, we must help our brothers and sisters see how much more beautiful and compelling justice is when we start with God and his Word. With that in mind, let's dive in for our final session.

Watch

Play session 14, "Confronting Injustice—Conclusion." As you watch, use the outline below to follow along and take notes on key insights.

- **Social Justice B is not merely a different political persuasion, it is an entirely different religion.** We can see this in twelve points of contrast between Social Justice A and Social Justice B.

	Social Justice A	Social Justice B
1.	. . . brings us to our knees before Jehovah as supreme and seeks a justice that begins with giving God his due. "You shall have no other gods before me" is where Social Justice A starts.	. . . erases the Creator-creature distinction and downplays the divine image in everyone. As with Jezebel turning ancient Israel to false gods, it lays us prostrate before the false gods of self, state, and social acceptance.
2.	. . . brings unity by acknowledging our shared blame in Adam and our new identities "in Christ." Jesus destroyed the wall of hostility between Jew and gentile to make for himself "one man," uniting people from every tongue, tribe, and nation and making them ambassadors of reconciliation. Family and reconciliation, not intergroup warfare, is the Bible's model for Christian living.	. . . leaves us in a state of uproar, breaking people into group identities, telling the most damnable edited histories of certain groups, making every individual of that group an exemplar of that evil, and blaming our current troubles on them. The predictable result is tribal warfare, one of the worst ideas in human history and with a staggering body count.
3.	. . . offers us the fruit of the Spirit, such as joy, peace, patience, kindness, goodness, gentleness, self-control.	. . . generates a spirit of mutual suspicion, hostility, fear, labeling, and resentment.
4.	. . . champions a love that "is not easily offended."	. . . inspires in its followers a quickness to take offense.
5.	. . . sees evil not only in "systems," where we ought to seek justice, but also within the twisted hearts of those who make those systems unjust. All the external activism in the world will not bring lasting justice if we downplay our need for the regenerating, love-infusing work of God in the gospel.	. . . blames all evil on external systems of oppression, often assuming that any disparity is damning evidence of discrimination. It then makes activism against that discrimination a "gospel issue," often downplaying our need for repentance and saving grace.
6.	. . . assesses everyone of every ethnicity as guilty because of our group identity "in Adam." This guilt can be erased not by oppressed group affiliation but only by finding our new and deepest group identity in Jesus, "the second Adam." Rather than condemning people for ethnic or gender group identity, "there is now no condemnation for those who are in Christ Jesus" (Rom. 8:1).	. . . credits guilt on the basis of one's skin tone, condemning people because of their group identity. Individuals must then work off their "infinite guilt" by confessing their privilege and joining the Social Justice B mission to end all oppression as its leaders define "oppression."
7.	. . . confronts us with the humbling reality that our self-righteousness is like filthy rags and Christ is the only ground for our righteous standing.	. . . inspires self-righteousness; i.e., enables us to think, "I am not a bigot because I hold these particular views on social justice or am a member of this or that cultural identity group."

8.	. . . calls us to love God with our whole minds. This includes evaluating ideas on the basis of their biblical fidelity and truth value. It also includes acknowledging real oppression and listening well, while refusing to interpret all of God's world as a mere power play of oppressors vs. the oppressed.	. . . interprets all truth, reason, and logic as mere constructs of the oppressive class, encouraging us to dismiss someone's viewpoint on the basis of their skin tone, gender, or economic status.
9.	. . . teaches that the Creator defines our telos. The refusal to live within that telos brings oppression to ourselves and those around us. Real authenticity and freedom don't come from defining yourself and "following your heart" but from letting God define you and following his heart.	. . . teaches that the human telos (i.e., ultimate purpose and meaning) is defined by the creature and that anyone who challenges our self-defined telos is an oppressor.
10.	. . . envisions the male-female differences as "very good"—distinctions that can't be erased without losing something precious. It highlights the male-female sexual union within the covenant of marriage as the only proper and life-giving context for human sexual expression.	. . . sees "heteronormative" sexual and gender distinctions as oppressive and seeks to liberate all forms of sexual behavior and gender expression from such "cisgender constructs."
11.	. . . accepts the full humanity and worth of unborn image-bearers of God and calls us to love and protect women and their offspring who are exploited or terminated by the abortion industry.	. . . celebrates abortion as an expression of female liberation from patriarchal oppression, excluding the preborn from its circle of justice.
12.	. . . celebrates family and upholds the rhythms of self-giving within family as a beautiful and God-ordained signpost of Jesus and his relationship to the church.	. . . interprets the nuclear family as an unjust patriarchal system of oppression, a construct that must be abolished.

- **Don't assume that brothers or sisters who point to the reality of racism or sexism are automatically Social Justice B proponents.**

- **Here's my practical advice moving forward:**
    - ○ Worship weekly with people different from you.
    - ○ Find ways to do justice in your sphere of influence.
    - ○ Keep the gospel first and preach it to yourself daily.
    - ○ Link up with solid justice ministries.

> The world is trying the experiment of attempting to form a civilized but non-Christian mentality. The experiment will fail; but we must be very patient in awaiting its collapse; meanwhile redeeming the time: so that the Faith may be preserved alive through the dark ages before us; to renew and rebuild civilization, and save the World from suicide.[1]
>
> –T. S. Eliot

Wrestle

To better internalize and act on what you just watched, choose three of the five questions below to wrestle through as a group.

1 Write down the top two or three insights you gained from this session, and briefly share one with the group.

2 Can you think of any more differences between Social Justice A and Social Justice B that you might add to the list of twelve?

3 Do you know people who have been ensnared in Social Justice B whom you could pray for?

4 Now that you've completed this study, what would you say are the top two or three insights you gained from the last several weeks together? Share your number one takeaway from this series.

5 How will you live differently, having explored biblical justice and its twenty-first-century counterfeits? List three specific ways you will apply what you have learned.

Wrap Up

Close your final meeting in prayer.

Congratulations for completing the *Confronting Injustice without Compromising Truth Video Study*. May God, in his grace, empower you to do justice, love kindness, and walk humbly with him.

Thaddeus Williams

Notes

How to Use This Study Guide

1. Cathy Newman, "Jordan Peterson Debate on the Gender Pay Gap, Campus Protests and Postmodernism," Channel 4 News, January 6, 2018, YouTube video, 29:55, https://www.you tube.com/watch?v=aMcjxSThD54.
2. Francis Schaeffer, *The God Who Is There* (Chicago: Inter-Varsity Press, 1968), 127.

Session 1: What Is "Social Justice"?

1. Jonah Goldberg, "The Problem with 'Social Justice,'" *Columbia Daily Tribune*, February 6, 2019, https://www.columbiatribune.com/story/opinion/columns/2019/02/06/the-problem -with-x2018-social/6085533007/.
2. See Thaddeus Williams, *Reflect: Becoming Yourself by Mirroring the Greatest Person in History* (Bellingham, WA: Lexham, 2018), 123–25.
3. See Francis Schaeffer, *A Christian Manifesto* (Wheaton, IL: Crossway, 2005); Kyle Harper, *From Shame to Sin: The Christian Transformation of Sexual Morality in Late Antiquity* (Cambridge: Harvard University Press, 2016); Rodney Stark, *The Victory of Reason: How Christianity Led to Freedom, Capitalism, and Western Success* (New York: Random House, 2005); and Brian Tierney, *The Idea of Natural Rights* (Grand Rapids: Eerdmans, 1997).
4. See Ian Barbour, *Religion and Science: Historical and Contemporary Issues* (San Francisco: HarperCollins, 1997), 3–32.
5. See Tom Holland, *Dominion: How the Christian Revolution Remade the World* (New York: Basic, 2019); and Thomas Sowell, *Black Rednecks and White Liberals* (New York: Encounter, 2006), 112–23.
6. "Three Reasons to Have Hope about Global Poverty," Barna Research Group, April 26, 2018, https://www.barna.com/research/3-reasons-hope-global-poverty/.
7. David O'Reilly, "A Study Asks: What's a Church's Economic Worth?," *Philadelphia Inquirer*, February 1, 2011, https://www.inquirer.com/philly/news/religion/20110201_A_study_asks __What_s_a_church_s_economic_worth_.html.

Session 4: The Idolatry Question

1. Camille Paglia, "Feminism. In Conversation with Camille Paglia," interview with Claire Fox, Institute for Ideas, November 4, 2016, YouTube video, 47:50–48:30, https://www.youtube.com /watch?v=4y3-KIesYRE.

2. Andrew Sullivan, "America Wasn't Built for Humans," *New York Magazine*, September 18, 2017, https://nymag.com/intelligencer/2017/09/can-democracy-survive-tribalism.html.

3. Elizabeth Corey, "First Church of Intersectionality," *First Things*, August 2017, https://www.firstthings.com/article/2017/08/first-church-of-intersectionality.

4. "The New Moral Code: Barna OmniPoll, August 2015," cited in David Kinnaman and Gabe Lyons, *Good Faith: Being Christian When Society Thinks You're Irrelevant and Extreme* (Grand Rapids: Baker, 2016), 58.

5. G. K. Chesterton, *Christendom in Dublin*, in *G. K. Chesterton: Collected Works*, vol. 20 (San Francisco: Ignatius, 2001), 57.

6. David French, "When Christians Are Too Afraid to Hear Ben Shapiro Speak," *National Review*, February 4, 2019, https://www.nationalreview.com/2019/02/ben-shapiro-speaking-ban-when-christians-are-too-afraid/.

Session 5: The Collective Question

1. Robert Putnam, *Bowling Alone: The Collapse and Revival of American Community* (New York: Simon & Schuster, 2000), 331.

2. Lisa Berkman and Leonard Syme, "Social Networks, Host Resistance, and Mortality: A Nine-Year Follow-Up Study of Alameda County Residents," *American Journal of Epidemiology* 2, vol. 109 (February 1979): 186–204, https://doi.org/10.1093/oxfordjournals.aje.a112674.

3. See Thaddeus Williams, "Love," chap. 4 in *Reflect: Becoming Yourself by Mirroring the Greatest Person in History* (Bellingham, WA: Lexham, 2018).

4. Melissa August et al., "The Hundred Worst Ideas of the Century," *Time*, June 14, 1999, http://content.time.com/time/magazine/article/0,9171,991230,00.html.

Session 6: The Splintering Question

1. Tom Segev, *Soldiers of Evil: The Commandants of Nazi Concentration Camps*, trans. Haim Watzman (New York: McGraw-Hill, 1987), 80.

2. Cited in Anna Szilagyi, "Dangerous Metaphors: How Dehumanizing Language Works," *Dangerous Speech Project*, March 8, 2018, https://dangerousspeech.org/dangerous-metaphors-how-dehumanizing-rhetoric-works/.

3. Thomas Sowell, *Black Rednecks and White Liberals* (New York: Encounter, 2006), 112.

4. Sowell, *Black Rednecks and White Liberals*, 112.

5. Sowell, *Black Rednecks and White Liberals*, 113, 116.

6. Sowell, *Black Rednecks and White Liberals*, 117–123, 132.

7. Sowell, *Black Rednecks and White Liberals*, 117.

8. Sowell, *Black Rednecks and White Liberals*, 116, 126.

9. Sowell, *Black Rednecks and White Liberals*, 116.

10. Conor Barnes, "Sad Radicals," *Quillette*, December 11, 2018, https://quillette.com/2018/12/11/sad-radicals/.

Session 7: The Fruit Question

1. These four quotes cited in Elahe Izadi, "The Powerful Words of Forgiveness Delivered to Dylann Roof by Victims' Relatives," *Washington Post*, June 19, 2015, https://www.washington post.com/news/post-nation/wp/2015/06/19/hate-wont-win-the-powerful-words-delivered-to -dylann-roof-by-victims-relatives/.

2. bell hooks, "A Killing Rage," 2, accessed August 29, 2019, https://sjugenderstudies.files.word press.com/2013/09/killingrage-bell-hooks.pdf.

Session 8: The Disparity Question

1. Ibram X. Kendi, *Stamped from the Beginning: The Definitive History of Racist Ideas in America* (New York: Nation, 2016), 11.

2. David Kocieniewski, "Study Suggests Racial Gap in Speeding in New Jersey," *New York Times*, March 21, 2002, https://www.nytimes.com/2002/03/21/nyregion/study-suggests-racial-gap-in -speeding-in-new-jersey.html.

3. Thomas Sowell, *Discrimination and Disparities* (New York: Basic, 2019), 88–89.

4. Sowell, *Discrimination and Disparities*, 89.

5. Sowell, *Discrimination and Disparities*, 11.

6. See Lisa A. Keister, "Religion and Wealth: The Role of Religious Affiliation and Participation in Early Adult Asset Accumulation," *Social Forces* 82, vol. 1 (2003): 175–207, https://doi.org/10 .1353/sof.2003.0094; and Lisa A. Keister, "Conservative Protestants and Wealth: How Religion Perpetuates Asset Poverty," *American Journal of Sociology* 113, vol. 5 (2008): 1237–71, https:// doi.org/10.1086/525506.

Session 9: The Color Question

1. The Black Lives Matter organization was founded by self-proclaimed "trained Marxists." See Yaron Steinbuch, "Black Lives Matter Co-Founder Describes Herself as 'Trained Marxist,'" June 25, 2020, https://nypost.com/2020/06/25/blm-co-founder-describes-herself-as-trained -marxist/.

2. *Washington Post*, Fatal Force database, accessed July 16, 2020,https://www.washingtonpost.com /graphics/investigations/police-shootings-database/.

3. "Criminal Justice Fact Sheet," NAACP, accessed January 27, 2022, https://naacp.org/resources /criminal-justice-fact-sheet.

4. "2018 Median Household Income in the United States," United States Census Bureau, September 26, 2019, https://www.census.gov/library/visualizations/interactive/2018-median -household-income.html.

5. Joyce A. Martin et. al., "Births: Final Data for 2017," Centers for Disease Control and Prevention, *National Vital Statistics Reports* 67, vol. 8 (November 7, 2018): 12, 25, https://www .cdc.gov/nchs/data/nvsr/nvsr67/nvsr67_08-508.pdf.

6. Drawing on data from the US Census Bereau, Zenitha Prince adds, "While 74.3 percent of all White children below the age of 18 live with both parents, only 38.7 percent of African American minors can say the same." Zenitha Prince, "Census Bureau: Higher Percentage of

Black Children Live with Single Mothers," *Afro News*, December 31, 2016, https://afro.com/census-bureau-higher-percentage-black-children-live-single-mothers/.

7. "Barriers to Black Progress: Structural, Cultural, or Both?" Manhattan Institute, February 11, 2019, https://www.manhattan-institute.org/html/barriers-black-progress-structural-cultural-or-both-11751.html.

8. Sowell, *Discrimination and Disparities*, 116. In light of these facts, Sowell asks, if the continuing effects of past evils such as slavery play a major *causal* role today, were the ancestors of today's black married couples exempt from slavery and other injustices?

9. "Talking about Race," The National Museum of African American History and Culture, Smithsonian, accessed July 23, 2020, https://nmaahc.si.edu/learn/talking-about-race/topics/whiteness.

10. The addition of power to the definition of racism was first put in print in 1970 by Patricia Bidol-Padva, as "prejudice plus institutional power." A. Sivanandan, *Communities of Resistance: Writings on Black Struggles for Socialism* (London: Verso, 1990), 99.

11. Musa al-Gharbi, "Who Gets to Define What's 'Racist'?" Contexts: Sociology for the Public, May 15, 2020, https://contexts.org/blog/who-gets-to-define-whats-racist/, emphasis in original.

12. "Dallas Conference On-Stage Interview with Ekemini Uwan," sistamatictheology, April 7, 2019, 33:15, YouTube video, https://www.youtube.com/watch?v=G9JQntpn71I.

13. Thomas Sowell, *Black Rednecks and White Liberals* (New York: Encounter, 2006), 138–139, 168.

14. Sowell, *Black Rednecks and White Liberals*, 129.

15. Neil Shenvi, "An Anti-Racism Glossary: Whiteness," accessed August 1, 2019, https://shenvipologetics.com/an-antiracism-glossary-Whiteness/.

Session 10: The Gospel Question

1. *The Good Place*, season 3, episode 11, "Chidi Sees the Time-Knife," originally aired January 17, 2019, on NBC.

2. *The Good Place*, season 3, episode 10, "The Book of Dougs," originally aired January 10, 2019, on NBC.

3. Özlem Sensoy and Robin DiAngelo, *Is Everyone Really Equal? An Introduction to Key Concepts in Social Justice Education* (New York: Teachers College Press, 2017), 203.

4. C. S. Lewis, "First and Second Things," in *God in the Dock: Essays on Theology and Ethics* (Grand Rapids: Eerdmans, 1994), 280.

5. Conor Barnes, "Sad Radicals," *Quillette*, December 11, 2018, https://quillette.com/2018/12/11/sad-radicals/.

6. Elizabeth Nolan Brown, "Moral Outrage Is Self-Serving, Say Psychologists," Reason, March 1, 2017, https://reason.com/2017/03/01/moral-outrage-is-self-serving/.

Session 11: The Tunnel Vision Question

1. Vincent Rue et al., "Induced Abortion and Traumatic Stress: A Preliminary Comparison of American and Russian Women," *Medical Science Monitor* 10, vol. 10 (2004): 5–16, https://pubmed.ncbi.nlm.nih.gov/15448616/.

2. Rue et al., "Induced Abortion," 5–16.

3. Priscilla Coleman, "Abortion and Mental Health: Quantitative Synthesis and Analysis of Research Published, 1995–2009," *British Journal of Psychiatry* 99, vol. 3 (September 2011): 180–86, https://doi.org/10.1192/bjp.bp.110.077230.

4. See, for example, Sarah Owens, "I Went to Planned Parenthood for Birth Control, But They Pushed Abortion," *Federalist*, September 28, 2015, https://thefederalist.com/2015/09/28/i-went-to-planned-parenthood-for-birth-control-but-they-pushed-abortion/.

5. Micaiah Bilger, "Abortion Was the Leading Cause of Death Worldwide in 2018, Killing 42 Million People," *Life News*, December 31, 2018, https://www.lifenews.com/2018/12/31/abortion-was-the-leading-cause-of-death-worldwide-in-2018-killing-42-million-people/.

6. Clarence Thomas, "Box v. Planned Parenthood of Indiana and Kentucky, Inc." Justice Thomas cites George Will, "The Real Down Syndrome Problem: Accepting Genocide," *Washington Post*, March 15, 2018, A23, col. 1, https://www.washingtonpost.com/opinions/whats-the-real-down-syndrome-problem-the-genocide/2018/03/14/3c4f8ab8-26ee-11e8-b79d-f3d931db7f68_story.html.

7. Caroline Mansfield, Suellen Hopfer, and Theresa Marteau, "Termination Rates after Prenatal Diagnosis of Down Syndrome, Spina Bifida, Anencephaly, and Turner and Klinefelter Syndromes: A Systematic Literature Review," *Prenatal Diagnosis* 19, vol. 9 (1999): 808–12, https://doi.org/10.1002/(SICI)1097-0223(199909)19:9<808::AID-PD637>3.0.CO;2-B.

8. Clarence Thomas, "Box v. Planned Parenthood," https://www.law.cornell.edu/supremecourt/text/18-483. Justice Thomas cites Mara Hvistendahl, *Unnatural Selection: Choosing Boys Over Girls, and the Consequences of a World Full of Men* (Philadelphia: Perseus, 2011).

9. With data from a 2013 NYC report, Lauren Caruba reports, "Black women accounted for 29,007 terminated pregnancies, representing almost 42 percent of all abortions in the city. That same year, black women in the city gave birth to 24,108 babies. With abortions surpassing live births by nearly 5,000, African American women in the city clearly terminated pregnancies more often than they carried babies to term." Lauren Caruba, "Cynthia Meyer Says More Black Babies Are Aborted in New York City than Born," *Politifact*, November 25, 2015, https://www.politifact.com/factchecks/2015/nov/25/cynthia-meyer/cynthia-meyer-says-more-black-babies-are-aborted-n/.

10. "What We Believe," Black Lives Matter, accessed July 10, 2019, https://blacklivesmatter.com/what-we-believe/. In the face of mounting criticisms, the organization scrubbed this page from its website in September 2020.

11. Joyce A. Martin et. al., "Births: Final Data for 2017," Centers for Disease Control and Prevention, *National Vital Statistics Reports* 67, vol. 8 (November 7, 2018), 12, 25, https://www.cdc.gov/nchs/data/nvsr/nvsr67/nvsr67_08-508.pdf.

12. "Things Are Looking Up in America's Porn Industry," NBC News, January 20, 2015, https://www.nbcnews.com/business/business-news/things-are-looking-americas-porn-industry-n289431.

13. "Can You Guess 2018's Most Viewed Categories On the Largest Porn Site?," Fight the New Drug, July 9, 2019, https://fightthenewdrug.org/pornhub-visitors-in-2018-and-review-of-top-searches/.

14. "Can You Guess?," Fight the New Drug.

15. "Pornography & Public Health: Research Summary," National Center on Sexual Exploitation, August 2, 2017, https://endsexualexploitation.org/publichealth/.

16. Cristina Maza, "Christian Persecution and Genocide Is Worse Now Than 'Any Time in History,' Report Says," *Newsweek*, January 4, 2018, https://www.newsweek.com/christian-persecution-genocide-worse-ever-770462.

17. "Persecution According to the Bible," Open Door USA, accessed July 9, 2019, https://www.opendoorsusa.org/what-is-persecution/.

18. Jean-Louis Panne et al., *The Black Book of Communism: Crimes, Terror, Repression* (Cambridge, MA: Harvard University Press, 1999).

19. *Generation Perceptions: Victims of Communism Memorial Foundation Report on U.S. Attitudes Towards Socialism*, October 2016, 3–5, http://arielsheen.com/wp-content/uploads/2017/11/VOC-Report-101316.pdf.

Session 12: The Suffering Question

1. For Shai Linne's full story, see "George Floyd and Me," Gospel Coalition, June 8, 2020, https://www.thegospelcoalition.org/article/george-floyd-and-me/.

Session 13: The Standpoint Question

1. Thaddeus Williams, "Post-Postmodernism," *Journal of Christian Legal Thought* 6, vol. 1 (Fall 2016): 1–4.

2. Margaret L. Andersen and Patricia Hill Collins, "Reconstructing Knowledge," in *Race, Class, and Gender: An Anthology* (Belmont, CA: Wadsworth, 2012), 4–5.

3. Tyler Tsay, "What Happens Behind Closed Doors: Calling on Faculty and Administration to Dismantle Violent Structures," Williams Record, February 20, 2019, https://williamsrecord.com/2019/02/what-happens-behind-closed-doors-calling-on-faculty-and-administration-to-dismantle-violent-structures/, emphasis added.

4. Naima Lowe, quoted in "The Evergreen State College: Part Two: Teaching to Transgress," Mike Nayna, published March 6, 2019, YouTube video, beginning at 2:45, https://www.youtube.com/watch?v=A0W9QbkX8Cs.

5. James Cone, *Black Theology of Liberation* (Maryknoll, NY: Orbis, 2010), 61.

6. The only exception to the list I provided before is Thurgood Marshall, who served on the Supreme Court during the 1973 *Roe v. Wade* decision.

7. Nicholas Wolterstorff, "Why Care about Justice?," *Reformed Journal* 36, vol. 8 (August 1986): 9.

Session 14: Conclusion

1. T. S. Eliot, "Thoughts after Lambeth," in *Selected Essays* (London: Faber, 1972), 342.